The Sacred Ministry

The Sacred Ministry

EDITED BY

G. R. DUNSTAN

LONDON

S·P·C·K

1970

First published as a series of articles in Theology
(October 1967 to April 1969)
and reprinted in one volume in 1970 *by* S.P.C.K.
*Holy Trinity Church, Marylebone Road, London N.W.*1

Printed in Great Britain by
Hollen Street Press Ltd., Slough, Bucks.

SBN 281 02351 4

CONTENTS

NOTES ON CONTRIBUTORS

G. R. Dunstan is F. D. Maurice Professor of Moral and Social Theology at King's College, London, and a Canon Theologian of Leicester Cathedral; he has been Editor of *Theology* since 1965.

Basil S. Moss is Chief Secretary of the Church Assembly Advisory Council for the Church's Ministry, and an Honorary Canon of Bristol Cathedral.

A. K. Hamilton has been Bishop of Jarrow since 1965.

Sir Humphrey Mynors, an Honorary Fellow of Corpus Christi College, Cambridge, was Deputy Governor of the Bank of England until 1964.

Andrew Elphinstone was Rector of Worplesdon, Surrey, from 1953 to 1962.

A. A. K. Graham is Fellow and Chaplain of Worcester College, Oxford.

Ronald Preston is a Canon Residentiary of Manchester Cathedral, and Lecturer in Christian Ethics in the University of Manchester.

Alan Webster is Warden of Lincoln Theological College and a Canon and Prebendary in Lincoln Cathedral.

Helen Oppenheimer is a writer on moral and philosophical theology, and was until recently lecturer in Christian Ethics at Cuddesdon Theological College.

Victor de Waal was the Anglican Chaplain to Nottingham University when he wrote his essay; he is now Chancellor of Lincoln Cathedral.

Paul Burrough was, before becoming Bishop of Mashonaland in 1968, the Bishop of Birmingham's chaplain for overseas peoples.

Alan Ecclestone has been Vicar of Holy Trinity, Darnall, Sheffield, since 1942.

J. H. B. Andrews has been Vicar of Chittlehampton in the diocese of Exeter since 1946, and is a Proctor in Convocation.

J. Dominian is a Consultant Psychiatrist at the Central Middlesex and Shenley Hospitals, and a Roman Catholic layman.

INTRODUCTION

The essays in this volume were first published in the monthly journal THEOLOGY, between the autumn of 1967 and the spring of 1969. They are reproduced here as they first appeared, and in the same order. The series was introduced by the Editor of THEOLOGY in September 1967 (vol. LXX, no. 567), in an article in which he argued that, so many proposals for the reform of the Church of England—its constitution, institutions, and forms and places of worship—having been launched in recent years piecemeal, wisdom would dictate some scrutiny of their cumulative effect, if all or most of them were enacted. In particular he asked for some consideration of the nature and function of the ordained ministry as a necessary condition of finding proper answers to questions, already under discussion, about its "deployment". This concern dictated the choice of subjects for the essays, and of persons to write them. Inevitably there are gaps: partly because, with the best of advice, not every question could be asked; partly because a very few essays would not take shape in the minds of their would-be authors. Of those printed, all except two were commissioned. That of Sir Humphrey Mynors began as a paper read by invitation at a diocesan clergy school; Dr Dominian's was delivered as part of an address on a commemorative occasion at which the Editor was a guest, and he commandeered the script. The Editor would express his thanks to all the contributors, and to his advisers in the planning of the series.

The series occasioned some correspondence in THEOLOGY: the Reverend Paul King, Chancellor E. Garth Moore and the Reverend E. Kenneth Lee in particular criticized positions taken by the Editor[1]; the Reverend J. K. Byrom added an historical perspective to Mr Ecclestone's essay with a note on W. F. Hook's town ministry in Leeds[2]; and Mr (now the Reverend) K. L. Yates developed some of Canon Moss's thoughts on role in a sociological context.[3] Readers of the book may be interested to turn back to these pages in the journal.

It was known at the outset that the Ministry Committee of the Advisory Council for the Church's Ministry (ACCM) was pursuing a similar quest with the help of a working party. The Report of this Committee, entitled *Ordained Ministry Today*,[4] was published in March 1969 and reviewed editorially in THEOLOGY in May. It confirmed two at least of the

---

[1]THEOLOGY LXX, 570, Dec. 1967, pp. 554, 555; LXXI, 571, Jan. 1968, p. 276.
[2]LXXII, 586, April 1969, p. 179.   [3]LXXII, 587, May 1969, p. 214.
[4]Church Information Office, 1969. 43pp.

Editor's convictions: the first, that the common concerns of the Church and its ministry must engage the vigorous attention of "private enterprise" as well as of official committees; the second, that the parish priest, urban and rural, can still give a better account of himself than the official pen seems determined to give him.

Since the thirteenth century at least, and in some respects from four or five centuries before that, the foundation of the ministerial life of this country has been the commitment of a priest to a community, not, indeed, irrevocably, but with the intention and effect of establishing a relationship secure enough for the pastoral task to be accomplished. It is said, of course, that parochial communities are now ceasing to be, and repetition is assumed to make the statement true. But the evidence for it has not been presented, and perhaps the properly relevant questions have not yet been formulated. This is a subject for another book. While it is being written we may well reflect that a pattern of ministry, like a liturgy, is not useless simply because it is old: both the parochial ministry and the liturgy may prove more difficult to replace than to destroy.

THE EDITOR

I

The Sacred Ministry as a Learned Profession

G. R. DUNSTAN

I

The form of this paper I owe to an indiscretion. In a gathering of doctors, medical and other social workers and clergymen, where everyone was agreed (not surprisingly) that they ought to co-operate, I observed that co-operation implies *difference* between the co-operators: that it rests upon the supposition that the priest is not a doctor, not a social worker, just as the doctor or social worker is not a priest. If they exercised the same skills, if they occupied the same rôles, one could not complement the other. Therefore it was not only inappropriate, but also a hindrance to true co-operation, if the clergy assumed to themselves therapeutic or manipulative rôles which were not their own, or spoke of their work in terms borrowed from other disciplines: "soul-surgery" was, in fact, the term which provoked my indiscretion, but there are others. In short, the leading word in the historic phrase *cura animarum* means their *care*, or their being in *charge*, and not, as a work of human skill, their *cure*.

This, to me, is self-evident. I stand like Moses, shoes in hand before the burning bush, when I am in the presence of a thorough-bred doctor, or social worker, or priest. I suspect the hybrid. I affirm it to be a positive duty for a clergyman to deepen his insight and heighten his pastoral skill with valid knowledge wherever it may legitimately be obtained, including some psychological and sociological knowledge.[1] But the clergyman will not learn the right and most advantageous use of that knowledge unless he has such assurance in his own rôle as priest that he will not flirt enviously with those of doctor and social worker. Our immediate duty, as a condition of proper co-operation with men and women of other

[1] See Jean S. Heywood, *Casework and Pastoral Care*, SPCK, 1967.

professions, is to search out the ground, meaning, opportunity, disciplines, of our own.

This subject could have been approached in a variety of ways. I have approached it out of an interest, developed over the years when I was editing *Crucible*, in professional ethics; and more particularly out of a reading of Professor Dorothy Emmet's recent book, *Rules, Roles and Relations* (Macmillan, 1966). So, in my use of the word "profession" in this paper, I have in mind some words which she quotes of Professor R. K. Merton, on "the composite of social values" in the "concept of a profession":

> first, the value placed upon systematic knowledge and the intellect: knowing. Second, the value placed upon technical skill and trained capacity: doing. And third, the value placed upon putting this conjoint knowledge and skill to work in the service of others: helping. It is these three values as fused in the concept of a profession that enlist the respect of men.[1]

And in my use of the word "rôle", I have in mind Professor Emmet's own words,

> In a rôle one is a person of a certain kind put in a certain kind of relationship, and thus detached from purely personal idiosyncrasy.

And again,

> As a directive for behaviour in certain kinds of relationship (rôle morality) is structured by rules; if not by explicit and sanctioned rules, at least by implicit understandings, and maxims, or rules of thumb, as to how such a person would behave in this kind of relationship.[2]

The words of chief importance for our examination of the ministry as a profession are "systematic knowledge" and "trained capacity" in the first quotation; "a person of a certain kind" in the second; and "a certain kind of relationship" insisted on in the second and third. If we can work out around these phrases the ground of a clergyman's self-understanding, indeed of his self-respect, the further exploration of his professional activity, in Professor Merton's terms of "doing" and "helping", will be a relatively simple matter. The root questions concern the clergyman as a professional *man*.

II

The three key concepts, "knowledge", "person", "relationship", are inextricably linked in my picture of a professional man. I hope that the doctor to whom I may have to entrust a life – one of my family, or my own – will be a doctor *tout à fait*: "a certain kind of person"; that is, a man formed into a doctor by the exercise upon him of the medical *knowledge* which he has been acquiring since he was at school and which he is acquiring still; by trained *capacities* derived from his teachers and from

---

[1] Quoted, op. cit., p. 162 n.   [2] p. 158.

the daily exercise of his medical practice; and by his *relationships*, those with his colleagues in the profession of medicine among others. I want him to bring to his diagnosis and treatment what I may call "the medical mind"; I do not want the mind of an accountant, or of a golfer, or even of an evangelist, which turns itself marginally to this chance medical question – admirable as accountants, golfers, and evangelists are in their proper avocations. I want "a medical man", a member of *the* medical profession; a man whose whole pesonality will respond, in its several ways, to that human being who is before him, not simply as a man but as a patient; that is, in a professional relationship. In other relationships he is, of course, more than a doctor: at the clubhouse, the concert, in local civic or church affairs, without ceasing to be or acting other than he is – a professional man – he is "off duty" as a doctor and his responses and relationships are appropriately varied. The same could be written of the lawyer and "the legal mind"; and to some extent of other professional people also.

What now of the clergyman? The characteristic "knowledge" which must form him and his mind for his professional life can be none other than the knowledge of God; and that knowledge, in its systematic form, we call theology. Of course, this knowledge is given to all believers, lay as well as clerical: knowledge of God in Christ is the essence of Christian living; but the clergyman has to become something of a "specialist" in this knowledge, in a way which I shall suggest in a moment. Of course he must acquire other knowledge also if he can: of himself and other people, systematized into psychology; of the way people live and associate, systematized into sociology; of how, in a modern society, skilled help is brought to people in their social needs, systematized into social administration and social work. Of course he must acquire certain skills, liturgical, pastoral, social and domestic. But the knowledge character-istic of his profession, that which *forms* him as man and priest, must be the knowledge of God, articulated in, though always transcending, the various branches of theology.

Priesthood in the Christian church presupposes a doctrine of God, of creation, and of salvation. It presupposes a theological interpretation of the life, death and resurrection of Jesus. It presupposes a theological view of the society or community called the Church: that is, a belief about the continuing life of that community which cannot be described *only* in sociological terms. It presupposes certain actual, existential relationships between God and men, relationships which are actualized "in Christ" – that is, in relation to the person known in history as Jesus of Nazareth, theologically interpreted; and, as a consequence of this, certain relation-ships between men and men, similarly "in Christ". The primary function of priesthood, as I understand it – and by "primary" I mean that from which all others derive – is to symbolize in various ways these doctrines and relationships, and to be the focus or nucleus of their embodiment in

the local community of believers. In theological terms, the priest represents, gives expression to, activates, headship within that community of
believers which – similarly – represents, gives expression to, activates, a
specific local manifestation of that corporateness which we call the Body
of Christ.

He is, therefore, "a person of a certain kind" in response to vocation
and by formation – by the power exercised upon him continually by the
knowledge characteristic of his profession, the knowledge of God. He
stands in "a certain kind of relation" to a community of people, the
Church, and *ipso facto* to "the world" around, to which the Church stands
in a theologically defined relation and with a theologically defined purpose.
The "trained capacities" which the priest must develop are those which
will further his "doing", which includes his "helping" but is not confined
to it, in that dual relationship with "Church" and "world". His professional conduct is determined by his rôle – by the obligations imposed
upon him by what I called the theological presuppositions of his profession – and by the functions and expectations created by his relationship
with "Church" and "world". Given this concept of "rôle morality", let
him be as much a man as he will, as full a man, as bizarre a man, as much
a "character", as much a "personality" – and the more the better – yet
his professional conduct will be that of a priest – detached, in Professor
Emmet's words, "from purely personal idiosyncrasy".

My task here is to search out the ground of a clergyman's self-understanding, indeed of that in which he can find his self-respect, not to
pursue every particular of his professional activity. But if the ground
which I have sketched is recognizable as true at all, then it should be fairly
simple to follow out its professional implications, on the pattern, perhaps,
set out by Professor Emmet on pp. 158 ff of her book, or more fully in
her article in *Crucible*, October 1962. Among these I single out one: the
point of accountability. The professional man is accountable for the advice
he gives, even, in some professions, to the extent of liability to an action
in the courts for professional negligence. The accountability is, however,
a moral one, and not a civil one only. The professional man is distinguished
by his deriving from his professional knowledge certain professional
obligations: obligations to the "truth" which he knows; to the person –
be it client, patient, parishioner – consulting him; and to his colleagues in
the profession. In a clergyman these obligations are heightened: by the
particular nature or quality of the "truth" to which he is committed –
"saving" truth, in the old language; by the particular relationship in
which he stands to his parishioners; and by the particular sort of "service"
which they are to expect of him – not a "secular" service only but a
service derived from and governed by the Servant of God which is both
Israel the People of God and Jesus Christ, God's Servant-Son. Thus
theological truth, which is the characteristic "knowledge" of the clerical
profession, governs the characteristic activity of the profession, in content,

aim, method. Above all, theological truth integrates, makes into one "ministry", the many diverse activities of the clerical life. It has created, in the Church of England at least, the norm that the pastoral ministry is part and parcel of the liturgical ministry: that is, that the priest who goes about among his people as a pastor ministers to them also as priest, normally in their church, in word and sacrament: because the ministry of word and sacrament declares the *character* of the pastoral ministry; it creates the expectations; it sets out the ends – what the pastoral ministry is for, what it is to bring men to; and it determines the means, excluding what Professor Emmet called "personal idiosyncrasy", and excluding means proper to other professions, but not to this one.

III

The last point refers us back to the first, the ground of co-operation between the clergyman and a member of another profession, say, the doctor. The doctor pursues certain medical means towards certain ends, medically defined or understood. The doctor's training equips him to use those means: not merely by giving him certain manipulative skills, but also by forming him, moulding him, as a person, in such a way that he can contain and deal with the strains which the exercise of those skills throws back upon him. The surgeon is expected not to faint at the sight of blood; the psychiatrist not to become submerged under the waves of emotion which break upon him. Few clergymen nowadays are likely to attempt surgery. But some are tempted to play the psychiatrist: that is to say, to adopt the rôle, rules and relationships of a profession other than their own, for which they lack the appropriate professional training, in resistances as in skills. Others, similarly, find attractions in the rôle of the social worker. Dr David Martin, in his new book, *A Sociology of English Religion* (SCM Press, 1967), fired a warning shot about this – though whether the stricture latent in his words upon professionalism in social work is justified or not is debatable:

> Social work would frequently prove a most frustrating alternative to the professional ministry in view of the social worker's intense urge to professionalization and the inflated vocabulary accompanying that urge. As regards medical rôles of all kinds the attempt to maintain social distance with clients or patients generally precludes decent personal relationships. In other words, if [the] clergy wish to be pastors and friends, then they need to avoid any assimilation to professions which either have or seek to have a clinical ethos. In any case, why exchange one bureaucracy for another?"[1]

Be that as it may. We may not shirk the task of enquiring further whether these manifestations of interest – to say no more – in other professions are not evidences of a weakening of confidence in our own. If men today are apologetic about their priesthood, if they wobble in their self-respect,

---

[1] p. 121 n.

there must be a cause, and we ought to look for it. Dr Bryan Wilson has two chapters of his book *Religion in Secular Society* (Watts, 1966) particularly relevant to this question. In chapter IV he traces the "loss of presidency" by "religion" as such among other "social institutions" and activities, largely because religious diagnoses of and remedies for the world's ills have been replaced by scientific diagnoses and technological remedies. Even law and morals now pass beyond religious influence: the Churches are no longer arbiters of moral behaviour; they reflect it; they endorse, however tardily, changes which society itself has insisted on – e.g. usury, divorce, birth control, and the rest. At the parochial level, social welfare has become the concern of the State, and of other professions.

> Even in their pastoral functions, the clergy may be said to have lost influence, and to have become transformed, by the growth of specialists in social work, into amiable amateurs.[1]

We must note the implicit equation, in these words, of "pastoral functions" with "social work": if the equation is granted, the case is proved. But the whole purpose of my paper is precisely to question the assumption, and to ask whether the clerical profession has a characteristic function peculiar to itself or whether it can be exhausted in the functions of other professions, singly or together. We must note also that Dr Wilson, writing elsewhere – in his criticism of the Paul Report in THEOLOGY (Feb. 1965) – argued that the professional concept is ill suited to the clergy, and chiefly for the following reasons:

> The rôle of the priest is diffuse rather than specific. Of all social rôles the priest's calls for the widest use of his purely untrained capacities, and calls into play, more than in any other profession, his personality dispositions. Of all specialists – and he is one by virtue of his theological training – he is the one who in his rôle must use the greatest amateur abilities. In so many ways the successful priest is such, not because of his specific training and in terms of what he has been taught how to do, but because he has developed a lively sympathy, acquired a sense of tolerance, and because he is culturally informed and humanly committed.[2]

Despite the not unfriendly, indeed sympathetic, tone of these words, there is an evident divorce in the writer's mind between the theological training which makes the clergyman a specialist, and the well-developed human qualities, with no necessary relation to theology, which are the means to his "success". Theology is thus *unrelated* to the pastoral task. The divorce, indeed, may lie not only in Dr Wilson's mind: he may have observed it in our practice; if so, his words may not lightly be dismissed.

Chapter 5 in Dr Wilson's book is more specific. It is entitled "Secularization and the Clerical Profession" and it traces the decline in social status enjoyed by the clergy in the community. The facts cited are probably irrefutable; their interpretation is open to question; and, of

---

[1] p. 51.   [2] op. cit. pp. 96–97.

course, trends noticed may conceivably be arrested and indeed reversed. One sentence goes to the heart of our problem:

> Clerics have now come to disbelieve in the ultimacy of any answers which they can supply about social questions, as they did earlier about physical questions. [1]

In other words, as a profession we have come to disbelieve in the knowledge characteristic of our profession, or indeed that there is any such knowledge. The debate on the self-understanding of the clergy, and so of their rôle in co-operation with people of other professions, will not advance a step until we can decide whether or not, by and large, any such statement about us is true.

So far we have two alleged or contributing causes to the weakening of clerical self-confidence: a decline in public expectation, in the sense of society's no longer wanting what it thinks the Church has to offer; and a change in the social status of the clergyman co-incident with a change in his own theological belief, insofar as it concerns the pastoral ministry. A third cause may be sought in the personal formation of the clergyman himself. Even the best of psychiatrists – perhaps because they are the best – sometimes cannot bring themselves to accept a particular person as a patient: they know what they would have to handle if they did, and they know, in an honest assessment of themselves, that they could not cope with it adequately if they tried. Such a judgment can merit only our highest respect: it sets in relief the high standard of personal fitness demanded by that sort of work. (I am not speaking simply of moral fitness: I am speaking of professional aptitude in terms of the total intellectual, emotional and spiritual strength of a man, as the necessary condition of his exercise of technical skill.) Now suppose that the standard of this total professional aptitude were to fall in the profession of psychiatry generally: it would follow that many more patients, even the less seriously disturbing, would not be treated, or would be treated less well, and that the standing of the profession would inevitably decline.

Over-boldly, perhaps, I apply this by analogy to the sacred ministry. Earlier I reflected on the words "a person of a certain kind" which Professor Emmet used of a professional person in general, and which I applied to a clergyman in particular. Traditionally the Church has set great store on the formation of "a person of a certain kind" to be a clergyman. I set up "the priestly man" in parallel with "the medical man" – one whose profession could hardly be disguised, disguise himself sartorially as he might; and this because his profession was part of him; he wore the stamp or character of it in a more than formal sense. It may be that in the intellectual and spiritual confusions of our time we lack not the means only but also the intention, even the wish, to form such a man. It may be that part at least of the cult or exaltation of the layman in the

---

[1] p. 74.

contemporary Church derives from a failure in our vision of the person and function of the clergyman. In revulsion from the sanctimonious we perhaps discount the sacred; and so we are left with one word, "ministry", and – egalitarians all – we can find no meaning in it which everyone cannot share. If this be so, if the coming Church is to be left with a clerical body possessing no distinct, characteristic, knowledge or belief, and no distinct professional character, then, I suppose there can be only one answer to such a question as this: What ministry has a clergyman to offer to a given parishioner whose ascertainable needs are being met satisfactorily by other professional attendants, the medical by the doctors, the social by the social workers, the legal by the lawyers? What has the clergyman, as clergyman, to say to such a man? The answer, surely, can only be, on this supposition, Nothing at all. So I plead again for knowledge, "sacred knowledge", as the distinctive, characteristic and formative study of the sacred ministry. And lest I be thought to speak of head knowledge only, I quote some words from Dr Ulrich Simon's new book, *The Theology of Auschwitz*:

> The priestly contribution is the sacred knowledge, theology itself, pursued to maintain a constant state of sanctity. This theology, however, is no longer an academic study but the mental content of sacrificial living offered to God through Christ.
> It is not at all surprising that many clinical specialists welcome the dedicated priest who is not, and does not wish to be, a welfare officer. The secularization of the sacred person misconceives the task of reconciliation. The true interpretation of healing stresses the distinctive function of patient, doctor, and priest. To the last falls the responsibility of actualizing the atoning power which the Holy Spirit makes available to all by each
> The healing of men in society is our immediate concern, but the immediate concern is meaningless without the ultimate concern, and, as stressed before, the temporal cannot be enterprised unless there beckons the eternal vista of man made perfect in God.[1]

I know some of the answers which could be given to such questions as these, and to a discussion of the sacred ministry as a learned profession. However, I persist in asking these questions because I am not satisfied with the answers commonly given to them. Thanks to my teachers, I was given enough historical good sense to refuse either to idolatrize or to denigrate the clergy of earlier ages – patristic, medieval, Latitudinarian or Victorian – or to idealize their ministry and its reception in the so-called ages of faith. I am afraid I do not believe the philological and historical nonsense which translates "parson" or *persona* into "the person" of the parish: the parson was simply the rector, whether individual or corporate, present or absent, legally entitled to the great tithe, in distinction from the vicar who was entitled to the lesser tithe; no more. (Professor Emmet's chapter eight on "Persons and Personae" is far more to the point.) Neither do I believe in the myth of the squarson, from whose alleged ubiquity

---

[1] Gollancz, 1967, pp. 128, 148 f., 149 f.

reformers now seek grandiloquently to deliver us. I am not trying to identify the clergyman of to-day with any set rôle belonging to the past: though I would claim that what I have said of him has represented roughly his daily duty ever since there have been clergymen in England – and *normam vivendi docere* has been one of the tasks which Church and nation have expected of him from the beginning, until yesterday. Rather have I sought to interpret his ministry in strictly contemporary terms, in terms of professional rôle, of a particular form of ethical and economic association which developed into its present form in nineteenth-century England and which is extending to more and more functioning groups every year.

I am well aware that the professions are constantly under fire. Bryan Wilson, in the book to which I have referred, writes that

> the clergy, in common with other professions, have become concerned about professional solidarity. . . . The clergy increasingly recognize their *professional* allegiance, and this, necessarily, at some cost to their *denominational* allegiance.[1]

On this thesis, oecumenism, led by the clergy, becomes (with clinical theology, amateur sociology, liturgical reform and the rest) another compensation for waning social influence and position: we must close the ranks, because the very exercise of closing the ranks gives us something to do: it staves off, for a few years more, professional death. I am aware of this criticism. Yet when I look around to enquire where there are groups of people corporately engaged in ethical thinking – shewing signs of ethical life – it is in the professions that I find this happening: and who else is doing it? In some, the old etiquette is being brought up to date. In others, medicine in particular, there is debate on the ethical worth of the possibilities given by new techniques; and, in so far as the viewing, listening and reading public are brought into the debate, the nation is being given by this means something of the feel of ethical judgment and decision. (It may be that this sort of extension of what begins as a professional concern may be one way of breaking down the ring fences of group or class morality, about which Professor Alasdair MacIntyre has written recently in his *Secularization and Moral Change*.)[2] In thus using the language of the professional rôle for my interpretation of the sacred ministry, I hope I may be understood to be thinking, therefore, in terms suitable for a ministry for today. I recognize that the terms are not comprehensive. A profession carries with it certain social and economic rewards, though the professional man, properly, does not measure the service which he gives on a basis of equivalence with them. For theological reasons the priest may have to identify himself more than other professional men with totally unrequited service, even with depriva-

[1] p. 173 f. cp. Ian Linden, "Church, State and the Vietnam War," in *New Black-friars*, Aug. 1967, p. 597.
[2] OUP, 1967.

tion and suffering; though he is by no means alone in this respect.

I have one more protest to meet: it is that man is bigger than his rôle, and woe betide us if we ever seek to confine him to it. I hinted at my reply to this, early in this paper, when I described the ideal doctor or priest as a doctor or priest *tout à fait*, yet more than a doctor or priest. And Professor Emmet has pointed out (p. 149) that within existing traditions, new rôles are created, or the image of existing rôles is changed, by the impact of "great men" or exceptional individuals upon them: she instances Florence Nightingale, Dr Arnold and Benjamin Jowett. One could instance Hook of Leeds for the town parson, Samuel Wilberforce for the bishops, and Bennett of Chester for the deans. (It is easier to seek instances from among the dead!) Tradition, rightly understood, is not a prison: it is are generating power, calling up new men to give new form and opportunity to old rôles. It is required only that the men really believe in what they are.

2

Mapping the Ministry

BASIL S. MOSS

On all sides, it seems, there is a demand for succinct and authoritative statements or restatements of the nature and role of the ordained ministry. What are clergymen for? What is the job of the priest? of the bishop? What precisely is their standing and authority? What is the meaning of ordination?

To give a few obvious examples, in the Church of Rome one of the fruits of the second Vatican Council is the short decree *De Presbyterorum Ministerio et Vita*, which is being followed up by fresh discussion as the dearth of vocations is debated.[1] Short statements about the ministry are a common feature of the growing literature of proposed schemes of Church union from all over the world.[2] Ecumenical explorations are exemplified by the continuing and as yet largely unpublished exchanges in the Faith and Order Department of the WCC.[3] The British Council of Churches has published *The Shape of the Ministry*,[4] a report which has not yet received the attention it deserves, and the Scottish Churches Council has just produced *The Ordained Ministry and Training for it: the basis of a study document*.[5] Within the Church of England, the new constitution of ACCM (April 1966) has set up a Ministry Committee charged with "keeping under review different forms of ministry by men and women, ordained and lay", and with "promoting discussion within the Church, so far as this may be practical, about the adaptation of its ministry to meet the changing pastoral situation". One of its working parties is briefed to

[1] "Decree on the Priestly Ministry and Life," CTS, 1966.
[2] E.g. sect. 4 of *Towards Reconciliation* (Anglican–Methodist Unity Commission, 1967, SPCK).
[3] e.g. Concept X, November, 1965.
[4] First issued 1965, reprinted 1967, by the BCC.
[5] Obtainable from Scottish Churches House, Dunblane, Perthshire, and shortly to be published by the BCC.

produce a short statement of "the Nature and Role of the Ordained Ministry". [1] Similar "domestic" groups are at work in the Methodist and other British churches. Meanwhile, individuals do not cease to prophesy. [2]

Debate about the ministry is as perennial a theological theme as the authority of the Bible, or the doctrine of God. Nevertheless the present outburst of activity has obvious contemporary causes: the pressure of the ecumenical movement to re-examine and resolve if at all possible the "cold war" inherited from the Reformation; the fall in supply of candidates to the traditional full-time ministry, in all the "main-stream" churches, engendering questions about "recruitment policy" and the "image" of the priest's job; the equally widespread reappraisal of ministerial education and seminary training; the awareness of problems set by changes in the social context within which the ordained ministry is exercised; and (most fundamental of all) shifts of emphasis in the church's understanding of itself. Under the last necessarily foggy heading I include convictions and intuitions "in the air" which are intensely real for many people as they reflect upon their experience – such as that "the Christendom era" is over for the church (however much confusion there may be about what is taking its place); or that the forms and opportunities of lay participation in ministry are of fresh and exciting importance ("the age of the layman has arrived"); or that certain experiments in (say) East Harlem or Holland or some church situation nearer home are pointers to new "missionary structures of the congregation". Such things link up with continuing debate about the theology of the church. Whether welcomed or not reflections and experiments of this kind command wide attention and inevitably sharpen the questions about the ordained ministry.

This is an exploratory article for map makers rather than yet another exercise in map making. I want to pursue or at least to open up questions of language and method, which might be relevant to *any* of the current attempts to redefine, reanalyse or reassess the ordained ministry of the church.

When people ask for a short definitive statement about the nature of priesthood, or ask what a man is ordained to do, what kind of answer is expected? what kinds of answer might conceivably be given? What "interests", arising out of the particular task (e.g. institutional church reform or ecumenical negotiations) or perhaps out of the psychological stance and emotional involvement of the questioners, need to be declared? By what criteria (*a*) do we distinguish the more from the less meaningful and relevant questions? (*b*) the more from the less satisfactory answers? In particular, how do we evaluate the use of key-words to elucidate by classifying (priesthood is a "learned profession"; a "form of leadership"), or by providing models or images ("servant", "shepherd")?

---

[1] Cf. also "Further Thinking about the Ministry" (ACCM, March 1966).

[2] E.g. J. A. T. Robinson, *Meeting, Membership and Ministry* (Prism Pamphlets, 1966).

THE WAY OF SIMPLIFICATION

One very common and attractive way of mapping the ordained ministry is to try to find the simplest, briefest descriptive phrases. A conflation of the various definitions in this style known to me (they all overlap) would run:

General

1. The ordained minister *gathers, builds up, enables, equips,* or *leads,* a church community.
2. He *represents,* or *personifies,* or *embodies* the whole church in Christ, in the things he does: he *links* in his person the local church to the great church: he acts with *representative authority* in both church and world.

Particular (according to opportunity and tradition)

3. He preaches, teaches, interprets the Gospel.
4. He administers the sacraments and takes responsibility for ordering worship.
5. He exercises some degree of oversight, responsibility, care and rule.

The terms are the simplest possible, bearing obvious meaning for Bible student, theologian and general reader. They can be made to fit practically any church situation in time or space. This style of map-making is therefore particularly attractive to ecumenical and world-wide gatherings. It gives a plain framework (a map of the Underground?) for those who feel themselves otherwise hopelessly confused. But its achievement is at the expense of dodging most of the questions that people want to ask. Most of us need more maps in the atlas than the map of the world on page one. People still want to know what kind of authority and what degree of authority is referred to, how ordination is to be understood, what participation in these activities belongs to lay persons, and if so what kind of demarcation operates, and so on.

THE THEOLOGICAL AND SOCIOLOGICAL FRAMES OF REFERENCE

It belongs to the ambiguity of the church on earth that its functions and purposes can be construed in the language of faith, theology, revelation ("from inside"); while at the same time the church never ceases to be a social organization existing in this or that historical *milieu,* and as such able to be observed and analysed in terms of the way any human institution behaves ("from outside"). Any map-making about the ordained ministry beyond the way of simplification seems to me to involve these overlapping frames of reference or language-systems, which can be loosely labelled the theological and the sociological.

(a) *Theological map-work*

Both the interest and the difficulty of mapping the ordained ministry in theological terms spring from the fact that it has been acknowledged to be, and is desired to be, a "terminal of grace", a point at which the saving initiatives of God spark with men. In his ministrations the ordained man ministers in an authoritative way the work of Christ, whether in Word, sacraments or pastoral care. The map-work then turns on describing theologically what he does and making explicit the nature of his authority. Is the key to his ministerial acts a high doctrine of the ministry of the Word? Or is it possession of a "power of sacred Order, to offer sacrifice and forgive sin" (Council of Trent)? Or is it that he simply acts in the name of the church, the Body of Christ, which corporately does what is done, in the power of the Spirit? Or is it personal exercise of a charismatic gift, acknowledged by the church? Is his authority as an agent of divine acts simply recognized by the church at ordination? Or is it conferred upon him in the laying on of hands with prayer, by the commissioning church? Or is a link back to the apostles or to the undivided church ("apostolic succession") a necessary guarantee of his authority and an indispensable clue to its meaning? Christian history is littered with passionate disagreement on the answers, but all have agreed on the importance of the answers, which seek to safeguard this or that understanding of the reality of the mystery of God's activity breaking into the present.

The traditional way of settling these questions is either to appeal for an *ex cathedra* solution to the final court of Scripture or Tradition or else to develop arguments from history. The latter tend to start from the co-existence *ab initio* of the church and the ministry as of divine institution and significance, and then to seek to show that the one theologically depends upon the other, or that both are interdependent. The NT and early church history particularly are racked for evidence.

I simply want to draw attention to one feature of this way of mapping the ministry which is often neglected, the presupposed view of the nature of theological truth. The *ex cathedra* solutions clearly presuppose a "deposit" view. The "interpretation of history" line of argument commonly assumes that truth is disclosed in a "linear" way, with a chain of precedents always controlling the answer to the present question. This needs more justification than it normally gets, in discussions of the ministry. (I leave aside the interesting question whether it would be possible to defend treating clarification of the ministry and the church differently from other doctrines.) Quite a different approach, and one no less respectful to faith and the mystery of God's activity, might be to make the *present* experience of the church pose the questions about ministry which we ought to be asking. The arguments of the church in the past would not cease to be relevant, but would cease to prescribe the debate. We should be more free to admit to what extent *all* theological discourse is conditioned by the social *milieu* in which it takes place, and that so much of the classical argument about ministry reflects the age of "Christendom" which ran from the later Roman Empire to the very recent past. In fact, the coupling of "lay" with "ministry" of which the Editor of THEOLOGY complained recently[1] is being forced upon the church by its missionary obedience in present conditions, as is experiment with "part-time priests", and new priestly functioning in new social contexts. We have to choose how our theology is to be "earthed", whether (to change the image) to force our questions to fit the Procrustean bed of earlier answers, or to force the answers to fit the questions as they arise for us.

(b) *Sociological mapwork*

(In calling it "sociological" I am using the word as a general signpost, neither excluding the theologian's concern, nor claiming the precise universe of discourse belonging to the professional sociologist.)

An increasingly common element in mapping the ministry is to take for granted the sheer conservatism of the church, and to concentrate on analysing recent changes in society, and the challenge they present to the inherited ways of church and parson.[2] The old orientation was towards "the world we have lost"; the new must be towards "the secular city".[3] I think this approach is of obvious value, and needs no further comment. Much more neglected is analysis "from outside" of the church itself and its ordained ministry. I shall discuss the usefulness of this for our map-making under the headings of (1) "enabling the church" and (2) "acting as a representative", which have already appeared in the simplified map above.[4]

1. Humanly speaking, the church, like any other social structure or organism, has purposes which it seeks to fulfil, and problems to be solved of cohesion, maintenance and efficiency. If it is accepted that the leadership or management (typically the ordained ministry) has the functions of "building up" or "enabling" the church, what are these functions, as analysed from a sociological angle?

A widely-used tool in this field is "Operational Research".

> If we construct a model of an organization, it is possible to examine the way in which the model would behave if it contained within it the stated values or objectives of the organization being examined; and to compare this with what actually happens.
>
> Classic examples of organizations using wrong objectives are some of the American railroads, who came to think of their task as operating and running trains, instead of providing transportation which was the more basic and realistic

---

[1] THEOLOGY, September, 1967. The idea, of course, occurs in a Prayer Book Collect for Good Friday. [What we now read into this Collect is one thing; what its author and translator intended by it may be another. *Editor.*]

[2] E.g. *The Shape of the Ministry*, pp. 1–15; Basil S. Moss, *Clergy Training Today* (SPCK), 1964), ch. 2.

[3] Cf. Peter Laslett, *The World We have Lost*, Methuen, 1965; Harvey Cox, *The Secular City*, SCM Press, 1965.

[4] In these sections I owe much to Dorothy Emmet, *Rules, Roles and Relations*, Macmillan 1966, chapters 7–9: but the application to the church is my own.

goal they had started with. They thus dealt themselves out of the short-haul market to the benefit of the road hauler, by failing to adapt quickly enough, and entering the road haulage field when it was relatively easy to do so. Similarly, in business organizations, various departments may have objectives which are clearly defined in the eyes of the departmental head, and yet be misaligned with reference to the objectives of the whole organization; in fact the main problem of every organization is one of determining its sub-objectives in such a way that an optimum solution to them produces an optimum solution for the whole organization's aim.[1]

Applying this to the church, we might want to say that its aims as a social institution are (a) mission, meaning evangelism (propaganda?), and the influencing of the society in which it is set: world-ward; (b) worship and living out the life of the Gospel (in which case the life of the church, as the Body of Christ, is its own end): God-ward. These aims are of equal importance, and cannot be stated, of course, without using theological terms. Together with them exist convictions in the church about how they ought to be achieved and how they are being achieved.

The sociological commentator then sets against this the church as it is in reality structured and organized. He accepts the fact that there are different versions, not only because of the historical divisions of the churches, but because it has adapted itself in some measure to different social contexts in various parts of the world. He also accepts that churches are to different degrees prisoners of history. He asks analytical questions about the sort of structure a church is, and the sort of management it has, measuring them against its avowed aims.

The church evidently, in all traditions, feels that its aims are most intensely felt and realized at the *local* level, with embarrassing problems of cohesion and administration arising whenever its catholic or world-wide reality and cohesion are taken seriously. At these levels the problems of keeping the church together, and orientated to its aims, are qualitatively different. So is exposed a piece of cartography which is commonly neglected. What is a bishop (or a moderator) functionally considered? How far *in fact* is the local ordained minister his delegate or subordinate? At the local level, what kinds of leadership and collaboration between parson and people *in fact* "enable" the church? What kind of participation in decision-making with a view to fulfilling the church's aims actually takes place? These questions, it must be insisted, are factual before they are theoretical and are to be pressed against the immediate social and cultural context that the church is facing.

Besides the necessary tensions between the "top" and the "bottom" of ministry, this kind of approach highlights the tension at all levels of "management" between maintenance of the institution, with inevitable conformity to the present and the past, and creative responses in accordance with the aims believed in. In times of stability, the conflict between

---

[1] H. D. Dunn, "Social Change and Operational Research", *The Listener*, 3 February 1966.

the two, so important in mapping the functions of the church's leaders, is less acute than in times of social change.

Lastly, such an approach is likely to expose the reality for the church's ministry of "lower motivations" – e.g. power and the need to be a success – which may work for or against the overall aim. If the vicar in the country has a roof and six gargoyles to support, the vicar in suburbia often feels he is running a supermarket in cut-throat competition.

2. A rather different light is thrown upon the ordained ministry when we turn from its functional to its "representative" character, as explored from a sociological rather than a theological viewpoint. The priest or minister fulfils a *role*. The term, of course, is drawn from the theatre, where a part or character is played by an actor: used of society, it denotes a formalized relationship, fulfilled by a person but in a style prescribed for him by the expectations of the society round him. Such a person is under pressure from within and without to fulfil his role by conforming to it and internalizing it. On the other hand, as existentialist writers have been quick to point out, personal integrity might have to be defined as *not* conforming to one's role.[1] A man might, of course, play a multiple role, or several roles (and experience conflict between them): most of us do.

Ordination certainly admits to a highly-charged role, in terms of fulfilling the office of a minister of holy functions. But (as has been said) the role-play is determined *in practice* by the expectations of society rather than by the interior convictions of the agent. Notoriously, we are moving from a situation of widely-shared and understood expectations of a priest in our society to a situation of greater confusion or incomprehension about the role. The varieties of expectation now experienced by the agent often give rise to severe conflict and uncertainty.

In his article last month, Professor Dunstan seized upon the learned profession as a strongly defined type of role-play, which with its emphasis on knowledge and trained capacity, professional ethics and membership of a professional élite enables the proper nature and function of an ordained minister to be mapped out: he is both distinguished from other professional men and classified with them. I would agree that this analysis usefully unifies actual features of the nature and work of priesthood as experienced in England during the last 200 years. But is it catholic, of universal application? (In Greece, the theologians are laymen: what are the clergy?) Does it fit the way the concept of "profession" is now undergoing change in Western society?[2]

I ask these questions to make a methodological point, rather than to quarrel with Dunstan's case. I believe that mapping the ministry is best done by exploring the mystery through a multiplicity of complementary models or images, rather than by taking one model and turning it into a

---

[1] Cf. Sartre on the waiter, quoted by Dorothy Emmet, op. cit., p. 153.

[2] V. J. Freytag, "The Ministry as a Profession", in *New Forms of Ministry*, ed. D. M. Paton, Edinburgh House Press, 1965.

definition. Only so can we be true to what is perceived in the church's actual experience in very different social situations, and relate it constructively and critically to the continuing attempts at obedience to the Gospel in the world.

CONCLUSION

The reader may have noticed that throughout my "sociological" section a recurring theme has been "what in fact happens or is believed" as distinct from what ought to, or used to, happen or be believed. At a time when God has quickened the conveyer-belt of social change on which we all live, this constant reference to "what cuts ice now" (theologically, our present obedience to the Holy Spirit) must continually control our attempts to clarify for ourselves the doctrine of the ministry: being joined with an equal control spring from the theological interpretation of the Gospel and its implications for the ministry. Only so can we avoid the charge of an unthinking and irrelevant traditionalism on the one hand or a "sell-out" on the other. The sense that we think we know what the ministry is must coexist with the sense that we have yet to discover what it can be now.

My other theme has been multiplicity of discourse. No doubt the search will continue with us, as with our fathers, for a key-concept or dominant model of the ordained ministry, a unified way of talking about it. But in a time of rapid change I believe we shall do better to keep relating our concept of the ministry to our experience of it, getting at the mystery by using a multiplicity of models and images. As in these days of new towns and motorways, and changes in land use and local government boundaries, we need lots of different maps of the same area, frequently brought up to date, and based as far as possible on actual survey.

3

The Priest
as a Man of Prayer and a
Teacher of Prayer

THE BISHOP OF JARROW

"To pray and to teach souls to pray – it is all, for given this everything else will follow." That is how more than thirty-five years ago Dom Bede Frost defined the work of a priest in his well-known book *The Art of Mental Prayer*. In saying this he was not only appealing to a tradition which went back many hundreds of years, but was also giving expression to a belief which was very widely held by the clergy of his own day. Many of them would have been the first to admit that they did not always live up to this ideal, but they were in no doubt about what they ought to do. The call to the ministry was seen first of all as a call to closer union and fellowship with God, and prayer was looked upon as the one thing needful. Their pattern of prayer naturally varied. For some their prayers centred upon the daily Eucharist, the careful recitation of the Offices and regular meditation. Others preferred a less stereotyped form and laid more emphasis on prayer meetings, Bible reading and a daily period of quiet. But all would have agreed that no matter how gifted in other respects a priest might be, and no matter how hard he might work, he could not exercise a fruitful ministry or effectively serve his people without the support and strength that came from a strong prayer life.

A great deal has happened since Bede Frost wrote, both in the world and in the Church. All this has left its mark upon the clergy and affected the attitudes which they bring to their work. They no longer accept without question many of the assumptions of their predecessors, and one way in which this shows itself is in their attitude to prayer. There seems clear evidence that the clergy to an increasing extent are finding the traditional patterns of prayer not only uncongenial but meaningless, and because of this some at least appear to give the impression that they have lost confidence in prayer altogether and no longer regard it as a pre-condition of pastoral effectiveness. The Archbishop of Canterbury has described this attitude as a spiritual sickness.

> "There is in this country", he said in a sermon preached at the installation of the present Superior of the Community of the Resurrection, "a strange sort of spiritual sickness. Sickness is, I think, the right word, as we often feel sickness and are damaged by it in body or mind without being able to identify it or be certain of its cause. The sickness in our Church is a sort of malaise of the soul, seen in a weakness in faith and a scepticism in prayer and a priesthood which tends to lose heart. So come the tendencies to clutch at remedies which are themselves part of the sick-ness, such as substituting psychological harmony for holiness or trying to justify the Gospel and the Church in terms other than the terrible loving kindness of God."

There is much in our contemporary Church life which bears this out. I suspect, for example, that the increasing interest which some clergymen are showing in social and welfare work, and the emphasis which is now being placed on Christian action in the secular world, are not simply due to the laudable desire to minister more effectively in Christ's name to the needy and the oppressed. They are due, in part at least, to a feeling that it is essential for the clergy to justify themselves to themselves and to other people. It is a modern version of justification by works. Unless a priest is meeting an obvious need or doing something which the man in the street immediately recognizes as useful, he may be tempted to assume that his work is valueless. All too rarely is there sufficient appreciation that, because man is made by God and for God, the greatest service one human being can do for another is to bring him into closer union and fellowship with his Creator.

Similarly, the impatience which a growing number of the younger clergy now feel with regard to the parochial ministry and the not un-common desire to opt out of this kind of work cannot be solely attributed to a very proper wish to criticize our existing parochial structures, or to a sudden appreciation of the importance of specialist forms of ministry, or even to the emergence of a new generation of clergy possessing the necessary gifts and qualifications for work of this nature. The cause of this is, I fear, due to some extent to a failure to appreciate that a parish priest, like every other priest, has a distinctive and special role to play. In an article in the October 1967 THEOLOGY it was suggested that it is necessary for a priest before all else to be wise in the knowledge of God because without that he would have nothing distinctive to offer or give to his people. Such knowledge will result only in part from a solid grounding in theology, for knowledge of God is not the reward of intellectual effort alone. It is above all God's gift to those whose lives are lived in union and fellowship with him. That is why a priest who neglects to pray or has ceased to give priority to prayer must in the end fall down on his job. For when that happens he is neglecting the principal means open to him of attaining to the knowledge of God which can alone enable him to perform the distinctive role which he has been called and commissioned to discharge.

Yet as always there is another side to the story. Alongside the scepticism in prayer which has received so much publicity there is evidence in many quarters of a wide interest in spirituality. The very fact that many people are finding prayer so difficult and the traditional forms of prayer so meaningless is seen not as an excuse to abandon prayer but as a challenge to seek for a new kind of spirituality better suited to the needs of modern man. In other words, it is possible to discover that behind the present impatience with our existing methods of praying there is a deep concern about prayer itself. Today, there is still a widespread realization that it is part of a priest's vocation to be a man of prayer but, at the same time, there is considerable uncertainty about how this may be achieved.

I do not claim to be able to resolve this uncertainty or to spell out in any detail what form this new spirituality for which we are seeking ought to take. All I wish to do at this stage is to say two things. First of all, I want to utter a word of caution. In our natural eagerness to evolve a contemporary spirituality it would be a thousand pities if we lost sight of the spiritual treasures which have come down to us from the past and which still mean much to many people. What is new is not necessarily better than what is old, and spiritual renewal may come from a rediscovery of what is of worth in the old as much as from the emergence of a pattern of prayer which is totally new. In planning our prayers, as well as in our teaching, we need to pay heed to the truth which Jesus was enunciating when he said that "every scribe who hath been made a disciple of the kingdom of heaven is like unto a man which is a householder, which bringeth forth out of his treasures things new and old".

And secondly, I should like to direct attention to three questions which bear on the present situation and which ought to be engaging our minds. It seems to me essential that we should think afresh about the nature and character of the God to whom our prayers are addressed; that we should ask ourselves what we hope to achieve when we attempt to pray; and, thirdly, that we should consider what bearing the world in which we live may have on the method of prayer we adopt. I will try to deal with each of these questions in turn.

To speak about the nature and character of the God to whom our prayers are addressed is to approach the very heart of the problem for many people's difficulties about prayer start at this point. The word "God" has gone dead on them. God has ceased to be a living reality, and the traditional terms which have been used to describe his character no longer convince. In recent years some of our more forward-looking theologians have tried to face this problem and their speculations have attracted considerable attention. Unfortunately, what they have said has done little to help the man in the street to pray better, not because they have been wrong to encourage us to find God amidst the manifold activities and encounters of our daily life, not even because they have laid insufficient stress on God's trancendency, but because they have made God seem too impersonal.

In the past, it has been belief in a personal God which has brought reality into men's prayers. When they prayed they believed they were addressing someone, that they were entering into conscious communion with a personal being who supported and sustained them and with whom they could enjoy a relationship of the same kind as a relationship between two persons. The same thing is no less necessary for us today if prayer is to have any meaning. Our inability to pray is directly related to our failure to appreciate that the God with whom we have to do has revealed himself to us as personal. Dazzled as we are by the wonders of the universe and the marvels of science, this is a fact which we may find difficult to accept but it is a fact which is made luminously clear when we consider the manner in which God has disclosed his nature and character.

Our knowledge of God has come to us very largely, if not exclusively, from Jesus, who is "the image of the invisible God". The image we see thus revealed is a personal image, for in Jesus God is manifested in a person. The significance of that fact can easily be overlooked and lost sight of. It does not just mean that this was the most suitable method God could devise for communicating the truth about himself to our limited human minds. The implications are more far-reaching and exciting than that. Because God has chosen to reveal himself to us in a person we are given the assurance that the power at the heart of the universe is a personal being. That is why it is not enough to think of God merely as our Creator, or as the first cause, or as the ground of our being. It is true, of course, that God is not just a person or like any other person, but it does mean that he is someone not something, someone who loves us and whom we can love, someone who can communicate with us and with whom we can communicate, someone whom we can get to know and to understand on a person to person basis. And prayer is the means of bringing this about. It is the way God has provided for us of entering into, and sustaining and deepening a relationship with him which is personal and intimate and real. It is the response which those of us are compelled to make who have seen something of "the light of the knowledge of the glory of God in the face of Jesus Christ".

But we cannot leave the matter there. If to be a man of prayer and a teacher of prayer it is first of all necessary for a priest to know God as personal, we are bound to go on to consider the nature of the response we are called upon to make. On this point I have only one thing to say. The response we make must be a conscious response. Prayer, from the human point of view, has always been thought of as the lifting up of the heart and mind to God. It is a conscious act, a deliberate effort on our part to give our whole attention to God to the exclusion of all else. How people set about this will naturally vary. Some people will wish to follow, either literally or metaphorically, the dominical precept and to enter into an inner chamber and shut the door. Others will prefer to start at the opposite end and to penetrate through the world to God. But whatever method is employed the whole exercise will be meaningless unless it leads on to a conscious meeting with God. The will, if not the heart, must be directed towards God. We cannot pray if we remain completely unaware of the God to whom our prayers are addressed.

God, of course, is with us always and not only when we pray. We are never beyond his presence. We meet him in the world and we meet him as we give ourselves in service to our neighbours, but at such times we are meeting him without knowing it. What distinguishes prayer from all other Christian activities is not that God is with us when we pray and absent when we are doing other things, but that when we are on our knees his presence is made known and a real meeting with him takes place. To claim then, as some do, that we cannot be more directly or immediately in touch with God than when we are giving ourselves in service to our neighbours is to lose sight of this distinction. We may be close to God always, but we are only in the fullest sense in touch with him when we are deliberately seeking him in prayer and consciously responding to his initiative.

The manner in which people can best make their response depends upon many factors, but not least upon the environment which to a large extent determines the pattern of their lives. I believe that much failure in prayer and one reason why people appear to find prayer increasingly difficult is because we have not taken this sufficiently into account. We have lost sight of the fact that under modern conditions the methods of prayer we have been teaching can only be put into practice with the greatest difficulty. Sometimes this is due to the strains and stresses any Christian must feel as he tries to put his faith into practice in this secular age; sometimes it is due to an inability to secure enough privacy or leisure for prayer in its traditional form to be possible; sometimes it is due to a tendency to look upon prayer as an activity which is quite unrelated to the ordinary business of living. But whatever the reasons one thing remains abundantly clear. A priest who wishes to help his people to pray must be more flexible in his methods and vary his teaching to fit the needs and the circumstances of those whom he is called upon to bring into closer communion and fellowship with God. So in one case he may suggest a regular system of Bible reading followed by a formal meditation, while in another he will advise some simple form of contemplation. Or again, one person may be encouraged to draw up a definite rule of life, worked out in considerable detail, while another will be introduced to the methods of Brother Lawrence and urged to dwell upon the thought of God's presence as he carries on with his ordinary duties. What is wanted is not a new kind of spirituality better suited than the old one to the needs of modern man, but a more flexible approach to prayer which takes into account the needs of individual men and women who happen to be living in the twentieth century. That is why the priest who is seeking to teach his people to pray would do well to keep in mind the maxim which Dom John Chapman used constantly to repeat, "Pray as you can and don't try to pray as you can't".

I have only one further comment to make. While methods of prayer and times of prayer must vary in order to suit different individuals and particular circumstances, I am old fashioned enough to believe that we shall be doing our people a grave disservice if we fail to remind them that a spirit of detachment and the habit of withdrawal are essential elements in Christian spirituality. If you study the Gospels, you will discover that the life of Jesus followed an ordered pattern, a pattern of detachment and involvement, of withdrawal and advance. There were the times when he went apart to give himself completely in prayer to his Father, and there were the times when he gave himself completely in the service of other people. It is a pattern which has distinguished the lives of countless numbers of God's faithful servants throughout the ages, and we shall discard it at our peril. Precisely because all the emphasis at the present moment is on involvement, it is all the more essential that the teacher of prayer should encourage his people to "go apart", not to escape from their responsibilities, but in order to renew their faith and to refresh their vision.

In the case of busy people, this advice may seem impracticable, but with care and forethought it should often prove possible for them to arrange a weekly period of withdrawal for prayer and spiritual reading, if anything more frequent is ruled out. And when even this is unattainable and an actual physical withdrawal is out of the question, people may still be taught how to rest in the Lord amidst the occupations and distractions of daily life. For all alike the advice of St Jerome holds good,

"Let there be study of the divine word, mingled with prayer and solid meditation on eternal things, that by this leisure thou mayest balance all the business of the other time. But we say this not to withdraw thee from daily life but that thou mayest learn and there meditate what a one thou oughtest to show thyself in thy daily life."

Let the teacher of prayer as well as the taught keep this constantly in mind, for to be a teacher of prayer it is first of all necessary to be a man of prayer. Because the spirit of prayer is far more easily caught than taught, the primary way in which a priest can lead his people to pray is by doing it himself. That is why I want to end this article by quoting a few sentences from a lecture delivered many years ago by Evelyn Underhill to a group of clergy.

"The priest's life of prayer, his communion with God," she says "is not only his primary obligation to the Church; it is also the only condition under which the work of the Christian ministry can be properly done. He is called, as the Book of Wisdom says, to be 'a friend of God and prophet', and will only be a good prophet in so far as he is really a friend of God. For his business is to lead men out towards eternity; and how can he do this unless it is a country in which he is at home? He is required to represent the peace of God in a troubled society; but this is impossible if he has not the habit of resorting to those deeps of the spirit where his presence dwells."

Those words contain a vital truth which no priest should ever lose sight of.

4

What I look for in my Parish Priest

HUMPHREY MYNORS

On one fateful day last year, my Bishop asked me to be one of three lay people who would speak on this subject, for five minutes each, to a gathering of ordination candidates. There they were, all wearing their "L" plates and ready to listen, for five minutes anyway, to anything that might bear on the high calling to which they were committing themselves.

That seemed a bit rash, at the time: but this is far more presumptuous – to go it alone, at greater length, in a gathering not of Learners but of Advanced Motorists. Let me begin by saying that I am under orders: that I have not asked for nor been offered advice from any quarter as to what to say: and that, as Quince said in his prologue, "If we offend, it is with our good will".

One thing more by way of introduction. What you will get from a layman on this subject depends not only on his knowledge and his piety, the shortcomings of which will be obvious as we go along. It depends also on his background and prejudice. It is therefore appropriate to record that my father and both my grandfathers and three of my seven uncles were parish priests, without distinction of preferment except that one of my uncles rose to the venerable condition of an archdeaconry. Thus born with the sound of church bells ringing in my ears, if I were to call myself a churchman it would be difficult to distinguish habit from conviction. At least I was brought up not to refer to the parsons of England as "the inferior clergy".

My paternal grandfather was rector for most of his working life of a remote country parish: and at his death he was succeeded by his elder son who had been his curate, the two of them working there for close on eighty years. My father was thought a bit of a radical when he went off to serve his title at St Mary's, Portsea. On the other side of the family, there was the Georgian vicarage where we used to stay with our maternal grandfather. I recall the family prayers, with the family sitting all down one side of the dining room and the domestic staff sitting all down the other. The novel smell of the breakfast coffee steaming on the sideboard was my first introduction to the odour of sanctity.

Such a background indicates prejudices that are intensely conservative: and I may as well admit to one at once. An upbringing in country rectories gives one a strong feeling for the parson being .the parson of and to everybody, not merely the minister of a "gathered" church. How this is done in a parish of 15,000 or 20,000 people, many of them living in high buildings and working elsewhere, I do not pretend to know: but the ideal should not be lightly thrown away.

Such a background also induces something of a sense of history, which is why I set it out at such length. That remote country parish is now united with two others. The site of that Georgian vicarage is now occupied by a building of many storeys. So in answering the question one has to look for what is true in a parish of 500 or 5,000 or 15,000 souls: and one has also to look for what is true through. time, in a period of rapid and continuous change.

Fortunately, you already know that the answer is unimportant. What matters is what God looks for in his parish priest. This needs no elaboration: it is just the touchstone of any attempt at an answer.

The first thing one looks for in one's parish priest is that he is a man of God. How can one detect this? It is not a matter of appearances or of external observances. One forms the impression, rightly or wrongly, from conduct, very often in things not in themselves important. There are diversities of gifts but the same Spirit, who will be manifested one way or the other.

Evelyn Underhill, talking about the fruits of the Spirit, puts it like this:

> St Paul says not that the spirit of love shall bring forth such suitable qualities as penitence, diligence, helpfulness, unworldliness [or] good social or religious habits, but that the real sign that God, the Giver of Life, has been received into our souls will be joy and peace: joy, the spirit of selfless delight: peace, the spirit of tranquil acceptance.[1]

Of course that was not written of or for parish priests alone, but of or for all good Christian men – the butcher, the baker, or even the banker. So it cannot in this context stand by itself. There must be one particular manifestation, the desire to make other people walk with God too: that is, the vocation of a pastor. Let us now look at some of the ways in which this works out in my parish priest, without attempting to put them in any sort of priority or logical order.

My parish priest enters completely into whatever activity he is engaged

---

[1] *The Fruits of the Spirit*, quoted in *An Anthology of the Love of God*, pp. 34 f.

on at the moment, and is felt by others to be doing so: and yet he remains in a sense withdrawn, uncommitted. He can go from a funeral to a football match, from a committee to a confirmation class, giving to each all he has, as though their concerns were the only thing that mattered to him. He can switch from one wavelength to another, as it were, at the turn of a knob.

Inadequate? Possibly, although it may do more good than he thinks: and sometimes he echoes the anguished cry of the examinee, "No time to finish". Insincere? – not a bit of it. The point about being withdrawn or uncommitted is not that if he worries about everything he will develop ulcers, or even a nervous breakdown; and end up seeking light duty in a south coast parish, with accommodation of course. It is the result of his being certain that the outcome of all his activities is in the hand of God. They may recur in his prayers no doubt: but if he worries over the success or failure of a particular activity, he is judging the success or failure of his ministry by its visible outcome. And who is he to judge of his ministry? There is One that judgeth: and when the eventual decision is handed down it may surprise him.

So my parish priest can be all things to all men: yet never gives the impression of "putting on an act". This spontaneity bubbles out in the small things of life as in the large: for my parish priest is interested in everybody and therefore in everything. That sounds a tall order: and it does not mean that he is knowledgeable about everything, but that there is no side of life from which he can completely sign off.

Any examples I may give are not imaginary, but are chosen with care from outside the diocese of Guildford. What are we to make of a parish priest who rings up his churchwarden and says: "I have just had the report of the diocesan architect. He says that that trouble in the church roof is much worse than you feared. This is nothing to do with me."

Whatever is meant by that fashionable phrase "The Priesthood of the Laity" – I sometimes hope they will not bring it in until after my time – it cannot be expected that the laity will manage without a lead. There is one place to which they naturally look: and if they get none, they are unlikely to take off. But my parish priest must be careful not to find himself sublimating a temporary sense of failure of mission by throwing himself heart and soul into the church roof. That would be commitment, in the sense we have already rejected. What he has to do is to recognize, in all humility, the responsibility of leadership: and lead his flock in the direction of the church roof, even if this appears to mean delay or frustration in his leading them in what he judges to be more important directions. If he does it well, leading them roofwards makes it easier to lead them heavenwards – excuse the old-fashioned language – even at the same time, although not by the exact route which he would have chosen, if left to himself.

Now Leadership is a quality that in secular life is notoriously in short supply. How can it be fair to expect my parish priest to display it? A leader in secular life may be supported by the power to give commands, to impose sanctions, to invoke the traditions and *esprit de corps* of the group which he is leading: in the finish, to distribute rewards. Little of this is at the disposal of the parish priest – no commands, no sanctions, no rewards: but this is not really what we are talking about. Leadership is the power to evoke the right response in other people: and the commands, the sanctions and the rewards are evidence not that it exists, but that human nature is seldom good enough to do without them.

Some parish priests I have known – not in this diocese, of course – have appeared to be not very good at this duty of Leadership. This is not to be ascribed to a lack of faith but possibly to a misunderstanding of the nature of humility. It is sad to see that the duty does not seem to be more explicitly recognized. In the Rules for the Representation of the Laity, the primary duty of the Parochial Church Council is defined as "to co-operate with the minister in the initiation, conduct and development of church work both within the parish and outside". Of its nature, co-operation must be mutual: but there is no word about the duty of the minister to co-operate with the Council.[1] Doubtless this is because these are Rules for the Representation of the Laity, not Rules for the Running of the Parish: but they do not bring out the nature of the co-operation, which is that of a leader with those whom he leads. The impression given is that the minister gets on with it: and the Council lend a hand when they are told – or find out on the bush telegraph – what he is up to.

My parish priest does not need to have this spelled out. He knows that every Response must be preceded by a Versicle: and he works with and through his laity, not breathing down their necks all the time, but ready with encouragement, advice or warning as may be needed. He does this without the aid of commands, sanctions or rewards, although he has of course the advantage of what I have called, in secular terms, "the traditions and *esprit de corps* of the group which he is leading". But he has another advantage, which can make him a more effective leader than either he or anyone else might suppose. His aim is to be able to say: "I am among you as he that serveth." He leads not from the front, and certainly not from behind, but from below. He is the servant who leads, the leader who serves: and this kind of leadership evades both the tests and the limitations of the secular world.

At this point, I hear someone murmuring: "This is all very fine; but you wait till the Bishop asks me to talk on 'What I look for in my Layman'. " Yes, indeed. I know from personal experience how lazy and unresponsive a layman can be. There are many devoted and workmanlike

---

[1] The Synodical Government Measure, 1969, at 6.2.(1), states that "It shall be the duty of the incumbent and the parochial church council to consult together on matters of general concern and importance to the parish". *Editor*

parish priests up and down the country who say the Versicle all right, and find all too few to join them in the Response.

Take one aspect of the problem. At one extreme is the parish where the population is pretty static, as in the old-fashioned country parish. By the time one has been three times through the able-bodied population and it always comes back to the few Old Faithfuls – where does one look next? At the other extreme is the parish where the population appears to turn over within say five years. Just as one has recruited a really first-class team, they begin to drop off. They retire to Somerset or the breadwinner's place of business is moved to Chelmsford – where does one look next? In between is every combination of the two. The one generalization that can safely be made about the Church of England is that every parish is a difficult parish.

My parish priest is well aware of this, but is not daunted by it. He is also well aware that the more "successful", to human eye, his ministry appears to be, the more difficult the parish is likely to become. His problem now is not simply that of bringing strangers to the knowledge of the love of God, but simultaneously that of deepening that knowledge in those in whom it has been implanted. It is never possible to tick off anybody as having been "done": any more than it is possible to strike through a name as being quite impracticable to "do". Fishing for souls is more like fishing for salmon than for less noble kinds of fish. The interest of the fish has to be aroused by the skill of the fisherman when it is not actually hungry.

This leads me to mention another quality by which is manifested that my parish priest is a man of God and a pastor – a certain quality of Steadfastness. He has his ups and downs: but he always comes back again, as though there were some Prime Mover inside him that goes on steadily all the time.

I have stressed this idea of leadership at some length because it is particularly relevant at the moment. Many changes are under discussion, in which the laity are being asked to assume an entirely new measure of responsibility. This is not the place to say anything about the merits of these changes: in many of them my parish priest and I are both at the receiving end. But the attitude of many of the laity to change is still exemplified by the action of my great-uncle, when it was given out in the church which he so regularly attended that the following Sunday the choir would appear dressed in cassock and surplice; and when they came in, the congregation would stand. (This was the high tide of the Oxford Movement lapping gently up a faraway creek in Suffolk.) My great-uncle was simply horrified: but his regular habits and the pressure of my great-aunt constrained him to be in his place, with much internal turmoil. When the choir appeared and the congregation stood up, my great-uncle rose very slowly to his feet, very slowly unbuttoned his overcoat – overcoats had a lot of buttons in those days – very slowly took it off and very slowly folded it and put it on the seat – by which time the minister was just into "Dearly Beloved". He had not realized that the church was so warm: and he could not be expected to take off his overcoat sitting down.

My great-uncle was quite ignorant of the reasons for change: anxious not to be false to his convictions: quite unable to distinguish between convictions and prejudices: and above all, determined not to accept responsibility or make himself conspicuous.

My parish priest knows that faced with these changes, whatever he may think about them one way or the other, he cannot sign off. Greater participation by the laity does not reduce his importance and responsibility: they are enhanced by it. It is not a matter of "Over to you, chum": nor on the other hand is it a matter of inducing the attitude of mind which says, "Oh, Vicar, you tell us what to say". This is a fresh opportunity to be at the same time leader and servant, both leading and serving the laity towards a better understanding of the nature of the Church of or the liturgy.

By all means let the laity have in mind what Geoffrey Clayton said to one of his synods at Cape Town. After some remarks specifically addressed to his clergy, he continued: "And, my brothers of the laity, remember that you too are soldiers in Christ's army, and that you cannot contract out of his war. Don't be too critical of your clergy. It is unlikely that your rector will have all the gifts of all the Apostles."[1]

Nevertheless, the more the laity participate, the more of a priest they want their parish priest to be. Obviously this does not mean a member of some priestly caste. Obviously he is a man as other men are: and yet a very special kind of man. They will need him to be even more, and more visibly, that very special kind of man.

In this special capacity there is a considerable element of the skilled craftsman, and my parish priest will need to become more and more skilled at his trade. As a craftsman he will have a tool bag. Are there any particular tools, and particularly any new tools, that I look for my parish priest to have in his tool bag?

To avoid any misunderstanding, it should be clear that to demand leadership is not to demand a great capacity for organization. A string of committees for parochial affairs is no more certain evidence that the job is being well done than a string of guilds for hearing masses. As regards personal organization, there are splendid parish priests with batteries of filing cabinets and card indexes and tape recorders: there are splendid parish priests with very little. It all depends on the man, and on the job which he has been sent to do. What I look for is that my parish priest should recognize that his is a skilled trade, but should never mistake means for ends.

[1] Quoted in Roger Lloyd, *The Church of England 1900–1965*, p. 505.

This idea can be generalized over a far wider field than card indexes or committees. The tremendous spread of education and training has opened to a child of promise all sorts of careers which were once virtually closed to him for lack of cash or caste. This desirable widening of the market for talent has been accompanied by a great growth in specialization. We have long been accustomed to expect professional qualifications in a doctor: we now expect them in a local government officer, a book keeper, even a hairdresser. And so one is constantly seeing demands for fresh qualifications in the clergy. The parish priest, we are told, must of course have a good understanding of the working of the welfare state: he must be able to take advantage of modern methods of communication and publicity: as a pastor he needs some understanding of psychology and psychiatry, and so on.

All this is not to be dismissed off hand: for after making all allowance for fashion, some of these tools will be useful from time to time. In all but one or two of these fields my parish priest must inevitably be an amateur, even an ignoramus. He cannot as easily as his forebears fall back on the comforting reflection that his place in the community is assured without the tyranny of acquiring qualifications: that he is after all the *persona*, as necessary and accepted a part of the social scene as the village constable and the village midwife, not to mention the squire. We are indeed a long way from what Owen Chadwick found in a Victorian book of etiquette: "One must never smoke without consent in the presence of a clergyman, and one must never offer a cigar to any ecclesiastic over the rank of a curate."[1]

But although his status is no longer so easily to be recognized, let alone so carefully to be respected, the prospect is not really so complicated, for this reason. In ordinary life, professional qualification may now be a necessary condition but it is never a sufficient condition. Those who count in a community, whether local or national in scale, no longer do so in large part by virtue of birth or status: but nor do they by virtue of technique, for this is but one constituent of the complex and elusive recipe for Personality. The qualification that I look for in my parish priest is not that of an almoner or a psychiatrist or a radio performer but qualification *as a priest*.

What this means was put to me in this form a few weeks ago by a young priest – not from this diocese. We had met by chance – I did not even know his name – and he said to me: "What I find most difficult about my job is that I need a double portion of grace – one for myself as myself and the other to pass on to some member of the flock who needs it, and doesn't know how to get it, and may in fact get it only if mediated somehow to him or her through me."

If we are all experts nowadays, then my parish priest – using whatever tools are available to him – is the expert on (I quote) "the divine influence which operates in men to regenerate and sanctify and to impart strength to endure trial and resist temptation". That is the definition in the *Shorter Oxford English Dictionary* of the word "grace". We are back where we started.

To say much more about craftsmanship would be impertinent. My parish priest knows well enough the difference between speaking quietly· and speaking inaudibly: between decent speed and indecent haste: between ordered movement and the slick formality of a drill sergeant: between mystique and mystery. He knows the virtues of sheer silence. But there is one subject on which you will expect me to say something – the Preaching of the Word – for it is an old and cherished privilege of the layman to criticize the sermon.

One of the classical masters who taught me at school went on retirement to a country living nearby. There on one winter Sunday evening, with a little knot of peasants crouching as near as they could get to the coke stove, he mounted the pulpit, gave out his text, and began: "Those of you who have been at Thermopylae will remember . . ." Nowadays he will more likely begin: "Those of you who were looking at 24 Hours with Cliff Michelmore on Thursday . . ." or something of the kind. The latter opening is perhaps to be preferred as nearer to the lowest common background of his hearers: but what matters is what comes afterwards.

In this field I look to my parish priest primarily for instruction, in the pulpit or out of it. Instruction covers a wider field than the scriptures for the day. For the right sort of audience it may cover what the Church teaches on such matters as abortion, birth control, divorce, homosexuality or woman priests – the order is strictly alphabetical – as soon as (I feel tempted to add) the Church decides, on some of these, what its teaching is.

But some things that fill the news columns are different; shall we say Viet Nam, Rhodesia, or the iniquities of the City of London or the Duke of Edinburgh? On such things my parish priest will tell me not what to think but how to think. He and I are both dependent upon the incomplete, even tendentious, reports that we get. The fact that, if I may say so, I may know more about one or two of these questions than he does should not silence him: but it makes it the more necessary to teach me how to think and pray about them – teaching in language that may be child-like but is not child-ish.

A counsel of perfection, perhaps: but do you remember Ronnie Knox's warning? He quotes from Milton's *Lycidas*, "The hungry sheep look up and are not fed": and points out that with a very small change of order it becomes, "The sheep look fed up and are not hungry".

But if my parish priest, like the rest of us, cannot know all the circumstances, does this debar him from ever denouncing what he judges to be flagrant injustice or open sin? Of course not, for we have no warrant for supposing that the Christian vocation is an entirely cosy affair. We have perhaps been rather lacking, of late years, in this prophetic aspect of the Church's mission. The clue may be found in the saying "Whom the Lord loveth he chasteneth". If I may adapt a Pauline phrase, my parish priest is the pedagogue, the trusted and responsible slave who brings us to Christ: and as such he has the duty to chastise us when we need it. But if he is filled with the Spirit of Love, they who are chastised can feel that this is because they are loved, not because they are not loved. So let there be candour by all means, but not rigour: bearing in mind that we cannot entirely escape the way we have been brought up.

To give one example of this last point, whenever I read of a parish priest seeking, for entirely proper motives, to refuse infant baptism unless the godparents are clearly what they are intended to be, I am reminded of the climax of my career as a multiple but very idle godfather. This was when I was co-godfather with a former Archbishop of Canterbury. The christening was in Lambeth Palace Chapel, and was taken by the Archbishop himself, who displayed considerable agility in saying "Wilt thou . . . ?" from one side of the font and answering his own questions from the other. In the middle of the proceedings the godmother next me whispered in my ear: "I don't think I ought to be here really: I'm a Roman Catholic."

This was not an early example of the ecumenical spirit. It was not until many years later that British European Airways took to ferrying Archbishops of Canterbury to and from the Vatican. But without seeking to defend present practice, as long as there can be such goings on in high places, I look to my parish priest not to initiate a far-reaching reform of the whole Church from within one parish. Rather let him act with charity as well as with firmness: and bear in mind first of all the exhortation of the Bishop, "to seek for Christ's sheep that are dispersed abroad, and for his children who are in the midst of this naughty world". In the midst of this naughty world, have mercy on us.

My prejudices are by now evident – and evidently inherited from my great-uncle. There is nothing in all this, may be, to entrap the young: but however much they may have changed in other ways, the young still retain one characteristic of the young of all epochs – the power to spot an adult who is sincere and who takes them seriously. It all depends on the pedagogue.

And of him I ask a lot – a servant who neglects none of my interests: a leader: a craftsman: a teacher: a man of candour and compassion – but in all these things and above all these things, a pastor.

In my father's study, hanging on the wall over his prayer desk, was a shepherd's crook. This was not in expectation of episcopal preferment. Indeed it was not that sort of crook at all, one of those long poles which suggest that the medieval episcopal pastime must have been otter-hunting. This crook had been the gift of a working shepherd – about three feet long, an ash handle simply turned with a curly brass hook on the end.

But it was beautifully balanced in the hand, so that it could be used like a rapier – now here, now there – catch as catch can. It was his badge of office.

At your ordination to the Priesthood, the Bishop spoke of the office as "both of so great excellency and of so great difficulty". You then were convinced of the excellency and he was reminding you of the difficulty. You now know of yourselves the difficulty: can you doubt of the excellency?

5

Priesthood and the Tension between Christ and the World

ANDREW ELPHINSTONE

If the Editor owed the form of his opening article to an indiscretion,[1] I owe the contents of mine to some kind of metamorphic mischance. When first the subject was given me, I thought I understood what it meant. Two or three months later I realized that I did not. However, such ideas as had come to me I threw into the melting pot; and now I feel rather like Aaron making his monumental excuse about the golden calf. The following, for better or worse, is what has emerged.

I

The essence of priesthood or ministry is a blend of conferred status and personal quality. This article is designed to explore the tension between Christ and his world and to study the personal qualities, rather than the conferred status, of the clergy as they embody that tension. The Church of England has struck a remarkable balance between the preservation of the essential body of Christian doctrine and the permission of personal freedom for its clergy to interpret this doctrine in terms of their own vision and nature. Doctrine has been enriched and kept soundly grounded in reality by this process. A distinctive kind of holiness and wisdom have been characteristic developments among the clergy, and people have been helped by seeing the Christian truth at work in personalities who

[1] See above p.1.

have made it their own and are still not too far removed from the ordinary paths of life.

Idiosyncracy[1] and private interpretation (for private is different from personal) have to be disallowed, as the XXXIX Articles are careful to insist with regard to scripture. They would not be capable of even mooting answers to the great questions and problems of the Christian faith, which has assumed its shape and expression over centuries in which divinely guided thought has been at work on divinely given revelation.

Personal interpretation by the priest is quite another matter, for it means taking the objective truth of the faith and making it his own in such a way that he can express it in its integrity yet through the unique medium of his mind, personality and experience. The world at large does greatly want to find such interpretations which are at once authentically spiritual and which make assuring sense of the huge hotch-potch of pains and pleasures, goodness and badness of which life so manifestly consists; interpretations which, hopefully, strike them as being "with authority and not as [of] the scribes", and therefore both carry and convey conviction.

Tension is an inward thing and its existence is generally largely concealed from the outside world. This is particularly true of "ordinary" tension, the stress that arises when what is and what one wants do not coincide. It is also true of the tension which the purpose of God in Christ places before fallen and resistant man. Naturally this applies to the priest as much as to anyone else and thus he has to be not only the personal embodiment of the tension, as the exponent of God's purpose, but also the discerning counsellor of the person in whom the tension is at work. For this he must have a true knowledge of God and a wide objective vision of the world around him as the arena of God's activity. To put it another way, his vision of the truth, rooted in the transcendent, must be brought to bear on the realities of the immanent so that everything is seen and interpreted in relation to the all-embracing, providential activity of God. This is as much as to say that there must be more than a touch of the prophetic in the Church's priestly ministry. It is no coincidence that these days are witnessing a renewal of interest in the meaning of the prophetic element in Christianity and an awareness of its necessity. One of the special characteristics of prophecy is the inspired understanding of the significance of present events and experiences, particularly of the painful and disastrous ones, in terms of the knowledge of God's nature and purpose, as they impinge on individuals and nations.

In the Old Testament it was often in times of confusion and crisis that the prophets were raised up to declare God's purpose, pronounce his judgment or reassure about his sovereign goodness. The increasing complexity of world events and the anxiety and suffering which are

[1] Above p.2.

attendant upon it are perhaps the background to the resurgence of prophetic thinking today. (I am not forgetting that the Christian past has seen prophetic times.)

The Christian knowledge of God has a source of significance profound and far-reaching beyond all comparison with that of the Old Testament in the incarnation of Christ, the atonement and transformation of suffering and death into glory. As the world progresses and the pressures on man's body and soul become more severe, so do the tensions in facing and accepting a God-interpreted universe. This source of significance in Christ has to be drawn on more and more deeply as providing a key to the tensions and difficulties of life lived in obedience to God. If a spirit of prophetic realism is absent from the presentation of Christianity there is the risk, even the inevitability, that people thirsting for the words of life will find an empty ecclesiastical shell where the spirit gives no life and the letter merely kills, where tensions are created by religious obligations which are more of yesterday than of the "today", where, alone, spiritual reality is experienced and appropriated.

II

"My thoughts are not your thoughts, neither are your ways my ways, saith the Lord. For as the heavens are higher than the earth, so are my ways higher than your ways, and my thoughts than your thoughts."

Tension, in the sense with which this exploration is dealing, is the stress which arises in the spiritual and moral centre of our being when what we want we must not have; or what we must we do not want to do; and when, in this dilemma, we are met by a personal moral influence stronger and more imperious than we, that is to say God in Christ instructing our conscience of what the Holy Spirit would have us hear and know. Less consciously it may exist where men and women, in their fallen apprehension of what is good and bad, right and wrong, pursue ends varying between the merely unwise and the mortally sinful which set up damaging tensions, as evil pulls against the righteousness of the image of God.

What we want is to follow the dictates of our nature with its long legacy of emergence from lower life-forms and of primitive instincts based on self-protection and survival. This nature, because of what we know as the fall, is vulnerable to the power of the devil who is committed, in a cosmic conflict, to the deflection of mankind from his final fulfilment in God. (I cannot go along with those who try to explain the passion and the whole ontology of good and evil while denying the existence of the devil.) Consequently nature finds it far easier to descend than to ascend, to pursue self-centred enjoyments and material securities, than to seek the strait and narrow way that leads to eternal life.

God's creative providence is a call to ascend, to abandon self, to press on towards a destiny of transformation into the likeness of God, far beyond the ken of our fallen vision, beyond our felt capability, beyond the safety of the known. Against this nature wars. We resist the claim of the Gospel because we feel that in yielding to it we shall lose our freedom (and in so doing we actually turn away from, not towards, freedom.) We kick against the pricks of the stringent demand to take up the cross, to repent, to forgive, to mortify ourselves and to self-give, to which the Christian life ever more deeply pledges us. One has only to consider the implications of the dual command to love God wholly and one's neighbour as oneself to realize what a debacle their complete fulfilment would mean for natural inclination and the instinct to put self first.

In its most radical form resistance lies in man's desire for independence from the sovereignty of God. The parable of the vineyard and the heir lays bare the truth: "This is the heir, come let us kill him and the inheritance shall be ours." Not only is there the concupiscence which would appropriate the vineyard but even more the desire to throw off the domination of a master. Man's desire for independence cloaks the ugly truth of his hatred of God's claim on his life: ". . . now have they hated both me and my Father." What God's claim involves is what theology calls dying unto self. This is what makes the aspirations of spirit a death-knell to fallen nature, a seeming foolishness, an imagined deprivation ("Lest having him I should have nought beside"); though, "to those who are being saved, the power of God and the wisdom of God". To this Christ calls whether by sudden conversion or by gradual growth.

Teilhard de Chardin has suggested, in *The Phenomenon of Man*, that every biological advance over the millenia has been achieved at the cost of prodigious effort. Perhaps this gives a clue about this further stage of progress, this new creation in which man, at the divine behest, struggles to pass into the sphere of kinship with the Creator. A colossal intrinsic tension is always at work in him by the very fact of his being of the earth earthy and yet drawn to this kinship with the Lord from heaven. In a world devoted to the pursuit of gain, comfort and pleasure Christ stands over against mankind as the living testimony that all human aims and activities are subservient to the gaining of eternal life. What, he asks, shall it profit a man if he shall gain the whole world and lose his own soul? Yet we long to gain the world and its multitudinous attractions; and so unworthy aims and false values draw us constantly into tension with the best interests of our souls.

The Gospel is a creator of tension in that we resist its claim upon us. It is, nevertheless, a releaser of tension in that it gives access to God and to his mercy, forgiveness and acceptance through Christ and in that "the truth shall set you free"; thus whatever may be the tensions at work in mankind, we observe the strange paradox that Christ invites the world to enter into the joy of its Lord, to lay hold upon the promise of eternal life, to accept the role of the flock to whom it is the Father's good pleasure to give the Kingdom; yet the world is reluctant to hear and resists with malice, anger and violence.

The more closely one observes and analyses the reason, the more plainly it emerges that it consists, in one form or another, in one area of sensitivity or another, of the fear of pain and suffering – either of being asked for more than we can do or of being deprived of more than we can bear. Here, in this vital human experience of pain which baffles so many minds and holds so many back from Christian commitment, there is more to be said than is the normal content of Christian teaching. The Church has been preoccupied with the doctrine of man as sinning and forgiven man (and none will deny that this is the central truth of the Gospel). It has possibly given too little thought to the creative function of pain in God's purpose and to the wonder of the phenomenon of suffering and victorious man.

III

Tension, then, is what results when our wills are faced with God's imperative and we see in the doing of his will the prospect of painfulness. Freedom from tension lies not in escaping the will but in facing the painfulness (which may turn out to be less or more than imagined) and in accomplishing what spirit and will demand. So, therefore, pain – and the tension it raises – is something which, when accepted, belongs to God, an experience through which God's redemptive dealing is actualized in us by a process of strengthening and refining. This is exactly what the life and passion of Christ have marked out and shown us. He accepted pain as part of created reality and was reconciled to passing through it himself, though in coming to that point he underwent the very greatest tension. Even he, as Hebrews tells us, was made perfect through sufferings. Pain, therefore, is no longer necessarily the ancient enemy to be escaped, but now (confirming intimations in the sphere of nature), through Christ, can become a creative part in the economy of God's providence.

Yet pain is still an enemy. First because it is in itself a nasty and some-times a horrifying thing and must in no sense be gloried in or exalted. Even though Christ accepted it for himself and made it redemptively his own, he alleviated it whenever possible as a sign of the coming of the sovereignty of God; and Christian love and mercy attempt to do the same. Secondly, pain is an enemy because by it the devil can and does intimidate mankind into disobedience to God. It is a truly important fact that pain – or the threat and fear of pain – underlies sin as a causative factor, as it also follows sin as its result.

C. S. Lewis in *The Screwtape Letters* made a highly illuminating point of the fact that the devil has never created or invented anything new: that his whole strategy depends on deceiving people into mis-use of existing realities created by God. This is a useful concept and throws light on the argument about the devil's use of pain. Both pain and pleasure are experiences occurring within the framework of created reality and both are potent forces which the devil uses as weapons in driving or luring human beings to do his bidding and so to defy God. At first sight it might seem that pleasure is the stronger motivating force and that the devil's principal intent is to induce the soul to sin by the prospect of pleasure. Yet it is not so. In the case of pleasure we have only to conceive a desire for it to become painful to visualize its non-fulfilment; and it is this which, in the last issue, is likely to tip the balance in favour of assuaging the desire. Equally where a possibly unpleasant action – say an apology or a confession – is called for, the devil can suggest that the pain attached to performing it will be too hard to bear or unnecessary to put up with. In either case it will be by the threat of pain that he will succeed in luring or deflecting the human will into the act of defiance or negligence.

Pain, therefore, appears as the most important single factor in the experience of mankind and determines conduct to a greater extent even than pleasure. It is this which gives to pain its crucial importance; for in pain the battleground lies between good and evil, between God and the devil. Either the outcome is the victory of the devil's intimidation causing one to shun the pain and refuse the obedience or it is the victory of grace enabling one to pass through the pain and follow the way which has opened the Kingdom of Heaven to all believers.

Such, in outline, is the nature of the hold which the powers of evil have over mankind by the use of or the threat of pain. No human has ever completely challenged this situation nor broken through this tension. Sooner or later fallen nature succumbs to intimidation and turns aside from the implications of total obedience. Only Christ has done so and in the confrontation with pain, with the sin which goes hand in hand with it and with the devil who holds the reins of both, he overturned the whole balance of the devil's power. "When a strong man armed keepeth his palace, his goods are in peace: But when a stronger than he shall come upon him, and overcome him, he taketh from him all his armour wherein he trusted, and divideth his spoils." He passed through pain to the very end of pain's power to destroy, which also means the end of the devil's power to deflect from obedience. Resurrection proved that pain is no longer the ultimate arbiter of conduct nor the devil the ultimate possessor of irresistible persuasion.

Thus in a universe governed by love, we have the strange mystery that pain has a more significant role and a more creative function than pleasure. Here Christian doctrine has answers to the anguish of human experience unknown in any other religion. It is seemingly paradoxical, yet true, that pain and love are inevitably linked together. It can even be said that in the economy of God's providence pain positively must exist because without the willingness to suffer, which is what above all characterizes love, love itself could not exist. Why, indeed, should the grandeur of the human make-up expect love without a capacity to bear suffering? Inevitably, therefore, it had to be through the medium of pain that Christ won love's forgiveness for man; for to forgive means precisely to bear the pain which sin inflicts without returning the pain upon the sinner, without the poison of grudge or the further propagation of evil by anger – in effect to bear the pain in unbroken love. The same is true of the forgiveness of man by man. Forgiveness is, therefore, the apex of the "alchemy" by which love takes pain from the devil's armoury and brings it into the resources of God's redemptive activity.

No wonder the devil drove hard to deflect Christ from that total confrontation which was to rob him of his ancient power. Had he succeeded and made Christ turn back he would have remained secure in his possession of pain as the all-victorious threat, still able to terrorize man into doing his bidding, still keeping his power as prince of this world. The tensions which assail our fallen nature are an indication of the power he still has and of the fact that until the final redemption we may only overcome them and pass through their painfulnesses in the power which Christ himself gives.

It was in the temptations in the wilderness that these issues were first faced, fought out and settled. Rejecting the temptation of trying to cure the world's ills at a superficial level, he set himself to master the ills at their source. This meant undertaking the direct confrontation with and conquest of the devil's power of evil both cosmically and in its special arena of application, the heart and will of man. There, where the kingdom of heaven is capable of being established, he would meet the malice, bear the transgressions and share the griefs, transforming them into means of new creation. When he said "I, if I be lifted up will draw all men unto me" can he perhaps have implied not only that all men would find in him their forgiveness and reconciliation with God but also that they would see and by grace make their own the overcoming of pain and anguish and the grasping of a wholly God-embraced interpretation of life?

IV

The priest is ordained to set forth God's true and lively word and rightly and duly to administer his holy sacraments. In word, above all, he must set forth the fact of Christ's triumph over the devil's preserves of pain and sin for this constitutes the true and living relevance of Christianity in every life in every generation. Pleasure, happiness and goodness need no explaining: pain and sin do.

The Church, whose symbol is the cross where this happened, too much preoccupied with sin, seems hardly able to make the pain of Christ relevant to the pain of moral tensions and to show that to escape the tensions leaves them intact and the moral victory and freedom not won. It seems, almost, to have lost sight of the crucial issue which the wilderness settled for Christ, the realization that only by the confrontation of evil and pain can evil and pain be overcome. Here the priest's own acquaintance with the wrestling which this issue involves, both in himself and in others alongside of whom he stands, is all-important. Without this his gospel must be shallow and incomplete, failing to make the engagement with the vulnerable centre where decisive conflicts are shunned or solved and where pain can hold subtle sway. Too often there are to be heard in Church superficially pious irrelevancies or exhortations such as that in which the baptism service rather disastrously describes our Christian profession. Too often the evangelical stress on justification and decision masks the absence of the idea of the painful progress towards sanctification while the more catholic prescription for sanctity, in all-too-defined bundles from cradle to grave, undermines the painful tensions of deep moral decision. Too easily, in other parts of Christendom, a sacrificing priesthood can become an alibi for a sacrificial one; because a conferred status of sacrificing priest, if it is unaccompanied by personal acquaintance with the experience of sacrifice and the dynamics of tension, pain and love, becomes a symbol without meaning.

For most, including the priest, progress towards sanctification comes, under grace, in the encounter with the very ordinary affairs of life and, within that encounter, a determined confrontation with the tensions and pains which meet the conscience in relation to things and people. For the priest in particular this discipline is likely to be more exacting and constant and should lead to a growing realism, akin to that of Christ's outlook, in his grasp of the significance of ordinary life and of the issues of eternal salvation. This realism will have three main points of reference.

First, an unequivocal insistence on the "end-product" of God's providence; that the whole purpose of our creation is kinship with God, a finished identity with the divine nature, beyond all that we can imagine or desire.

Second, a view of life rooted in incarnation which, in distinctive Christlikeness, recognizes unfearingly the indigenous goodness of things and the original righteousness of people and which teaches that eternal life has its origin here and now, that God is at work not only in ecclesiastical ways but in what we sometimes call the "secular" world which Christ saw, knew and loved.

Third, however, a recognition that "the whole world lieth in the evil one"; and may it be quite clear that this means open to corruptibility at every point, not indigenously or intrinsically evil.

This three-dimensional "depth of focus" should enable him to distinguish and teach a true proportion between the important and the unimportant, the permissible and the non-permissible, the serious and the light-hearted, so as to give people relief from as many tensions as possible while laying stress on those which really matter. Christ banished a multitude of tensions which in Judaism had gathered round the spiritual path. Religion tends to build up a subsidiary paraphernalia of mores and moralisms and the clergy have to be specially careful not to let these, or their own prejudices, arrogances and ignorances, create unnecessary tensions, turning people away because they see these things to have no valid substance – for the popular conscience is capable, under God, of making very shrewd assessments of what is true and valid. When unnecessary or unprofitable tensions are done away, then the adamantine streak, the refusal to permit the essentials of salvation to be compromised, will be the more heeded, valued and even welcomed.

The spirit of today, penetrating and analytical, is against – perhaps too much against – ecclesiastical formality and wants incisive answers to existential questions and the priest must have the clarity of vision to answer them. While some would say that under the attack on institutionalism Christianity is breaking up, others live in the certainty that we are moving into closer confrontation with reality, its tensions and pains and intimations of victory. By its interpretation of pain the Christian faith stands supreme over other religions and philosophies and, while suspected of being blinkered, is in fact the one possessor of reality and relevance. Pain is an integral part of this present dispensation and is beyond neither the permission of God nor the tolerance of man. Malcolm Muggeridge in his *Tread Softly* made the deeply significant remark that "Religion, wisely, assumes misfortune, and so survives, while earthly utopian hopes, which must be disappointed, soon perish".

From what has been said it follows that in my belief the priest's handling of the problem of pain is the most significant of his personal functions of interpretation. Unless he can explain pain as an intellectually and morally comprehensible part of God's design (and act in accordance with that understanding) he will not be giving an account of the faith which embraces the most universal and controversial fact of the world in which we live. "Western man" is conditioned by every kind of influence, not least by television and other advertisements, to reject the idea that hardness, discomfort and pain are tolerable concepts for our world, and this has the effect of making people think that they need not be encountered, that if God's way involves such things, it had better be left well alone – or watered down. Numberless people are in the absurd and tragic position of rejecting, or never testing, the idea of God because of the suffering they observe (or themselves endure) and so find themselves alone with the suffering and bereft of the faith which could make it explicable. Yet here, at the heart of the Christian religion, is the crucified Christ blazing the trail to freedom and victory and showing that these lie on the other side of pain and of the tensions which faith and obedience create. The priesthood, embodying the call to carry that freedom to perfection and that victory to completion, is there to show that the nettle of tension is for grasping and that pain is for passing through, towards sanctification and eternal life.

6

Should the Ordained Ministry now Disappear?

A. A. K. GRAHAM

"*Must* a name mean something?" Alice asked doubtfully.

"Of course it must," Humpty Dumpty said with a short laugh: "*my* name means the shape I am – and a good handsome shape it is too. With a name like yours, you might be any shape, almost."

The recent correspondence in THEOLOGY about the names "priest" and "presbyter"[1] and the report entitled *The Shape of the Ministry*[2] touch on a question similar to that discussed by Alice and Humpty Dumpty. The similarity between Humpty Dumpty and the Christian ministry extends further: it is no exaggeration to say that those priests and ministers who, like Humpty Dumpty, were confident about the meaning of their names and who thought that their ministry had a good handsome shape have had a great fall. Can they be put in their place again? Or need they? Or should it be in some other place? Or in no place at all?

In order to suggest an answer to these questions it will be convenient to discuss three factors which have contributed to present discontent concerning the theory and practice of the ordained ministry.

First, among those who are convinced of the need for some sort of ordained ministry, there is a reaction against authoritarian and hierarchical views of the Christian ministry. Either to regard the Church as dependent on the ministry or to regard Church and ministry as mutually inter-dependent may result, many think, in a distortion of the proper relationship between Church and ministry. Both these views derive ultimately

---

[1] Vol. LXX, No. 570, Dec. 1967, pp. 555–57; vol. LXXI, No. 571, Jan. 1968, p. 27.
[2] Report of a Working Party, issued by the British Council of Churches, 1965.

perhaps from the Lord himself; perhaps from the stress which St Paul laid, in his epistles to the Corinthians, on apostolic authority; from the figure, in the later Pauline epistles,[1] of Christ as head to the body the Church; and from the suggestion in Ephesians[2] that the ministry was given by the ascended Lord to the Church. Whatever their origin, these views have the effect of regarding the Christian minister as set over the Church to rule it, lead it, shepherd it: however humble and patient a servant the individual minister may be, these views of the ministry treat him as being in some respects intrinsically superior to the other members of the body. These are by no means the only views concerning the Christian ministry. There are others which perhaps derive ultimately from the figure, in Romans 12 and 1 Corinthians 12, of the body of Christ and the body of the Church being in some sense identical; those who hold these views tend to interpret Ephesians 4: 4 ff. as meaning that various ministries are to be exercised in, with and under the Church, rather than over the Church or over against the Church. While the view which regards the ministry as set over the Church is not representative of much modern thinking concerning the ministry, it is probably true that reaction against this hierarchical, stratified, authoritarian view has in fact led, in part, to a reaction against *any* theology of the ordained ministry and against *any* type of ministerial authority.

In another respect, reaction against certain views of ministerial authority has affected other views besides. In an age when it is difficult to "come at" ideas of the supernatural and when the transcendence of God is often thought to be incredible, it is not surprising that there are attacks on views of the ministry which present it as the mediator of supernatural graces *de haut en bas*. Put at its mildest, a generation which finds it difficult to make room for the idea of miracle will suspect the efficacy of priestly blessings and consecrations. If the priest cannot do that effectively, then what can he do that any Christian cannot do equally well? Perhaps, like God, the Christian minister is being "killed by inches, the death of a thousand qualifications",[3] and assertions about the particular and peculiar efficacy of certain ministerial actions will be "so eroded by qualification"[4] that they are no longer assertions at all. Not every view of ministerial authority exposes itself to this type of criticism, but the effect of such criticism on some theologies of the Christian ministry has resulted not only in toppling them from their wall but also in undermining the position of those which have occupied a lowlier status.

Secondly, there is a matter which is much more difficult to assess: the rôle played by clergy in society. In some quarters there is what one might

---

[1] E.g., Eph. 1: 22–23; Col. 1:18.

[2] Eph. 4: 4 ff.

[3] A. Flew, "Theology and Falsification", in *New Essays in Philosophical Theology*, edited by A. Flew and A. MacIntyre, London, 1955, p. 97.

[4] Ibid., p. 98.

describe as an aesthetic distaste for clergymen, who themselves share in this distaste. There is nothing new about this: as some parts of English life have been clerically dominated, there is an inevitable reaction. Today, however, many people, Christian and non-Christian, lay and ordained, regard ecclesiastical titles and distinctively clerical dress as anachronistic and, so, distasteful. The clergy are no longer looked upon as members of a separate estate: they are no longer regarded as socially superior to people engaged in some other professions and occupations: it is apparent that they are in many cases intellectually inferior to an increasing number of the people to whom they minister. The Church's views and pronounce-ments are not accepted any longer (if they ever were) just because they are the Church's pronouncements: they command a hearing and respect in so far as they are argued cogently, set out persuasively and lead to conclusions which appeal to the rational sense of the general public. Similarly, while the clergy themselves may still sometimes have some deference paid to them by reason of their office, they generally command respect only in so far as they are people of integrity and intelligence. The clergy can still fill the gaps in the social services and act as a kind of ecclesiastical counterpart to the "God of the gaps", but this cannot compensate for the fact that the clergy no longer figure prominently in the magistracy, no longer largely control primary education, no longer are responsible for poor-relief, nor do the Church's views on moral matters carry the weight that they once did. Humpty Dumpty has certainly come off his wall: what is to be done with him now?

Thirdly, some think that, as man has now "come of age", he no longer needs the institutional Church, or if the Church does prove to be in-dispensable, then it too must "come of age". The time is past, it is said, when the Church needed to be under tutors and governors. Even thinkers who emphasize the importance of Church and ministry tend to derive their theology of the Church and ministry from a blending of Pauline teaching about the body of Christ[1] and Petrine teaching about the priestly nation.[2] Has not every Christian been given an inalienable priestly status? Are not Browning's words about Saul applicable to every single Christian just as much as to the minister whose orders are said to be indelible

> " . . . though much spent
> Be the life and the bearing that front you,
>   the same, God did choose,
> To receive what a man may waste, desecrate,
>   never quite lose"?[3]

Some of those who take this line believe that they are pressing Pauline and Petrine insights to their logical conclusion: all Christians share as equals in a common priestly ministry. There is no need for a special ordained ministry to dispense sacraments, evangelize, instruct, organize

[1] E.g., Rom. 12: 4 ff.; 1 Cor. 12: 12 ff.   [2] 1 Peter 2: 5, 9.   [3] Saul XV, 10–12.

and shepherd. Such a ministry, it is thought, can be, a positive hindrance to the growth of the Church and of individual Christians. In modern society there are increased opportunities for leisure, a higher general standard of education, a wider spread of the experience of responsibility. All are said to contribute to the conclusion that clerical, ordained leadership of the Church has the effect of preventing the Church from being the Church: far from enabling the Church, it acts as a disservice to the Church, obscuring its nature and hindering the growth of its members. In many areas, it is claimed, congregational responsibility can now take over the duties which were formerly carried out by ordained ministers when there were fewer opportunities for leisure and a lower general standard of education. Those who think thus rejoice at the embarrassment of some of their friends (in the first group, above) who are trying to re-think their theology of the ministry: they feel only that this embarrassment has not yet become sufficiently acute. Similarly, the aesthetic distaste for the clergy shared by others (in the second group) is positively welcomed: they feel only that the distaste should grow yet more repelling. To return to Humpty Dumpty: having fallen off his wall, he should be neither reinstated nor pieced together again, but left where he is as a broken shell becoming emptier and drier.

Of these three factors which contribute to present discontent and embarrassment with the ordained ministry (in both theory and practice), the last seems to be the most important. Dissatisfaction with certain types of theology of the ministry need not affect all views of the ministry: equally, the present shape and tastes of society do not necessarily mean that the ordained ministry is either theologically false or outmoded in practice. The third group of considerations, however, respresents an attack on the theological status and validity of the ordained ministry *per se*.

Since one type of theology concerning Church and ministry is so much criticized nowadays, it may be prudent to start not from theological considerations pure and simple, but from a few simple historical observations. It is an undeniable fact that, from the time of the New Testament onwards, Christians have generally had some kind of ordained ministry: there is dispute about the shape and functions of this ministry during the apostolic and sub-apostolic periods; and in the period since the Reformation there has been dispute about the proper nature and rôle of the ministry in relation to the Church. Nevertheless, generally speaking, the great majority of Christians through the centuries has had some sort of ordained, commissioned ministry. For the moment it need not be argued whether or not this ministry has been of divine appointment or intention: it is sufficient to say that most Christians have looked to an ordained person for word and sacrament, for pastoral care and for leadership in the local church. They have found such a ministry, if not essential to the being of the Church *qua* Church, at least highly desirable and even necessary for the functioning of the Church as a worshipping, believing, redeeming society. An ordained ministry of some sort has been so nearly an universal pattern that it is worth while to consider the circumstances of those groups of Christians which have not found one necessary.

Three types, which partly overlap, immediately suggest themselves: the immanentist, the individualist, and the egalitarian. The second century saw the development of the pneumatic ideal: the gnostic was seeking for personal enlightenment and salvation. Some gnostic sects undoubtedly had some form of organization, but the general drift of the gnostic movement was individualist. Stress was laid on the individual's quest for intellectual illumination and spiritual perfection. Later in the century the Montanist movement represented another attempt to achieve the pneumatic ideal. It tended to substitute for the regular ordained ministry of the Church the authority either of the inspired prophet or of the spiritual man. In many respects the movement was egalitarian and anarchic in tendency: in Tertullian's later works[1] we find a view of the Church as a "spiritual" society, combined with a disdain for bishops, while Phrygia had been the scene of wild prophesyings and frenzies. Both wings of the movement drew attention to the authority inherent in every individual "spiritual" Christian. Purely immanentist views were probably not held in the early centuries: in the sixteenth and seventeenth centuries, however, emphasis on the inward Christ, the light within, the God in every man, was accompanied by strongly individualist attitudes and also by anarchic enthusiasm. While even the Quakers[2] have had ministers who were recognized, approved, or recorded (and could be disowned), the general tendency of these movements has been egalitarian and individualist: the priesthood of all believers and of each believer has received such emphasis that it has been thought to be incompatible with an ordained ministry.

Over against these three types which have tended to belittle the importance of the ordained ministry or to dispense with it altogether, the general mind of Christians has advanced a number of considerations. These correctives were given classic expression in the early centuries. In the face of a movement which was in all probability partly gnostic and individualist, Ignatius[3] asserted the importance both of the Christian ministry and also of membership of the visible Church: later in the century, in an attempt to counteract similar tendencies, Irenaeus[4] emphasized the necessity of a regular ordained ministry. Even before Ignatius, however, Clement of Rome[5] had attempted to deal with confusion in the Corinthian church; he had emphasized the importance of order and orderliness,

[1] E.g., *de exh. cast.* 7; *de pudicit.* 21.
[2] See R. M. Jones, *The Later Periods of Quakerism*, London, 1921, vol. i, pp. 120 ff.
[3] E.g., *ad Smyrn.* 8.
[4] E.g., *adv. Haer.* IV. xxvi. 2.
[5] See especially chapters 40–44.

and in close connexion with these principles he discussed the rôle of the ministers in the old and new covenants. A century later, in the face of the pneumatic pretensions and the anarchy of the Montanist movement, the Catholic Church as a whole came to recognize even more clearly the importance of a generally accepted and regularly ordained ministry. While none of the early fathers had to deal with immanentist teachers as such, we can find in both Ignatius and Irenaeus the outline of later developments. Both took their stand on the importance of history, Ignatius[1] on the reality of the Lord's life, death and resurrection, Irenaeus[2] on the historical development of the Christian Church: each in his way served to remind the immanentist that Christian faith is not rooted solely in the inner experience of the believer, but also in historical events to which the Christian in later centuries is linked by a chain of historical continuity. In connexion with historical roots and historical development Ignatius and Irenaeus regarded the ordained ministry (and, in particular, the episcopal ministry) of cardinal importance. In other words, one might suggest that the existence of some regular, ordained ministry in the Christian Church has had the effect of counterbalancing and restraining purely immanentist views, undue stress on the individual person and congregation, and the chaos and disorder which have accompanied egalitarian attitudes. In the past, an ordained ministry has been considered desirable and helpful in order to deal with excesses in these three directions; an ordained ministry may well be helpful today in these same three respects.

First, immanentist views are not at all unfashionable now. Secondly, intelligent people who find some meaning in Christian assertions often do not find it easy to accept the institutional Church, to stomach the "elementary" teaching given there, to accept the ministrations of an ordained person whose intelligence they do not respect: as the Church loses hold on some areas of society, there are thrown up individuals and scattered groups who find sense in Christ and Christian insights but have only tenuous links with the Church. Thirdly, there has been, in this century, an immense increase in the number and membership of enthusiastic sects. We are familiar with immanentist, individualist and egalitarian views in twentieth century guise, and if the past is any guide for the present, one may suppose that the existence of an ordained ministry can still act as some sort of corrective.

But are there no more positive recommendations which can be advanced in favour of an ordained ministry? It may help to prevent undesirable developments in the life of the Church, but is that all that can be said in defence of the ordained ministry in face of the allegation that it acts as a hindrance to the growth in Christ both of the individual Christian and of the Church at large? Having acknowledged that in the past it has

[1] E.g., *ad Trall.* 9.
[2] E.g., *adv. Haer.* III. iii. 1–4.

sometimes been such a hindrance, one would say that it need not necessarily be such and that it has within it possibilities of helping Christians both individually and corporately to respond the better to their vocation and obligations. The clue lies, as Canon Moss has suggested in his article in this series,[1] in the representative nature of the Christian ministry. The representative work of the minister may be said to fall under three headings.

First, he *displays* something of the total response demanded by Christ of his disciples to follow and obey. This display should be the result, not the intention, of his discipleship: the response of the ordained minister to his vocation is not made in order that he may provide an edifying example of renunciation. Equally, this element in the minister's representative work should not be taken to imply that radical decision and loyal obedience should not characterize the discipleship of every Christian: it does not suggest or sanction the double standard. It means that certain Christians publicly, unambiguously, with particular solemnity, at a mature age, renew that total dedication to their master which, no doubt, they made some years earlier and which should characterize the life of every Christian: as they reaffirm their discipleship in this public and solemn manner, they accept further particular responsibilities. These responsibilities are pastoral, prophetic and priestly: the pattern and model in all three fields is the incarnate Lord. Now, in the era of the Church, the Lord's pastoral, prophetic, priestly ministry is undertaken by his members, as opportunity offers, in their various occupations and circumstances. In addition, certain of his members are publicly commissioned to make explicit this threefold responsibility, to do particular work which is unambiguously pastoral, prophetic and priestly both towards their fellow churchmembers and towards those outside the Church as well. They are (or should be) "beacons"[2] of pastoral, prophetic, priestly concern and activity, displaying to both Church and world something of the Lord's own love and obedience. "By ordination a Christian becomes a sign of the Ministry of Jesus Christ in His Church."[3]

Secondly, he *enables:*[4] the explicit and clear display should have the effect not of laming the Church, but of enabling its members to see more clearly what is meant by Christian discipleship and to pursue it more purposefully. The minister's enabling influence can be felt in personal example and in the fact that he is ordained to full-time service. Moreover, his personal gifts can be developed by professional training so that he may enable the Church to carry out its threefold work more effectively. Its pastoral work may be better done if at least some of it is carried out by people who have had training and experience in fields where goodwill

[1] See above, esp. p.17.
[2] I owe this figure to the Principal of Cuddesdon.
[3] M. Thurian, in *Studia Liturgica*, vol. V, No. 3, Autumn 1966, p. 167.
[4] See Eph. 4: 11 f. (RSV and NEB).

and common sense are not the only qualifications. Some of its prophetic work may be more effective if done by people who have had opportunities over several years to study and to reflect. So far as its priestly work is concerned, public worship stands a chance of being more worshipful and edifying if it is led by a trained professional rather than by an amateur. In addition, certain ministers will have particular backgrounds or particular gifts which will make them suitable for specialist work in connexion, for instance, with education or hospitals, with the young or the disturbed. In carrying out such specialist work, the ordained minister will be enabling the Church to fulfil its threefold responsibility in his own specialized field.

Thirdly, he *involves* the whole Church in his particular activity. This element in representative work is given classic expression by St Paul in connexion with the death of Christ: "one died, therefore all died."[1] Ideally, the whole Church should be caring and proclaiming, worshipping and reconciling, but this cannot be effectively done only by Christians in the course of their daily occupations. Particular people are, therefore, largely set free from other cares and duties in order that their time and energy may be devoted to these ends. When the sick are visited by the minister, he comes not merely as a sympathetic individual, but as the agent and representative of the whole Church and so of the Lord who founded and commissioned the Church, leaving it a pattern to follow. The minister ought to have more time to pray than most Christians have: when he prays, he prays as a representative of the whole Church, and the whole Church is associated with him in his praying. When he explains the Christian faith to the enquirer, declares the penitent forgiven, consoles the bereaved, knocks on the door of a house unknown to him, he does it all as agent and representative of the whole Church and of the Lord in the Church. All this may be clearly seen in the circumstances of the parish priest's life. It is equally true of the specialist ministries mentioned above, and of others: the Night Minister appointed by the San Francisco Council of Churches involves with him in his work the whole Church which has commissioned him: the ordained minister working in factory, hospital or office as mechanic, doctor or civil servant involves the whole Church which has commissioned him and approved of his wish to work in this setting. The ordained minister involves the reputation of his Church and of his master: any credit or disgrace reflects not on him alone, but on the whole Church and on the Lord who stands behind it and empowers it.[2]

This approach may be acceptable to those who are already convinced with Dean Stanley that "all good history is good religion".[3] Yet "the

[1] Cf. 1 Cor. 12: 26 ff.
[2] 2 Cor.5: 14.
[3] Quoted S. H. Hooke, *In the Beginning*, Oxford, 1947, p. 147.

weight of historic precedent is authoritative, but it is not conclusive: the final criterion is the Word of God".[1] This suggests that the conclusive factor is the genuineness and completeness of each minister's self-dedication and obedience. Jesus sanctified, consecrated himself for others:[2] to similar self-consecration every Christian, and *a fortiori* every minister, is called. The authority of the minister will derive from the Church and from the Lord whose commissioned representative he is, but the authoritativeness of the minister will derive from the authenticity of his own self-offering, from the integrity of his own response to the developing demands of his call to be a pastoral, prophetic, priestly agent in today's world, from the living quality of his own self-consecration. The minister's influence ultimately will depend not on education, nor on social position,[3] nor even on the fact of ordination, but on the quality of his initial and continually renewed response to his vocation. "The mark of a saint is not perfection but consecration:"[4] this is as true of the ordained minister as it is of any Christian. Whether one is depressed about the comparative inadequacy of any Christian discipleship and witness, or by the comparative ineffectiveness of the ordained ministry in particular, the message of the gospel remains one of invincible hope. The Lord's self-consecration provides the pattern and means for each disciple's self-consecration.

If the rejoinder comes that this is but the mixture as before, the last word must be Humpty Dumpty's last word to Alice: "Wait till you've tried."

---

[1] Charles Smyth, in *The Genius of the Church of England*, by A. E. J. Rawlinson and Charles Smyth, London, 1947, p. 32.
[2] John 17: 19.
[3] Cf. 1 Cor. 1: 26 ff.
[4] Bishop Westcott, quoted J. B. Magee, *Reality and Prayer*, London, 1958, p. 175

7

The Priest
as a Teacher of Ethics in a
Plural Society

RONALD PRESTON

Our attention is specifically directed to the contemporary plural society. There appear to be at least three implications of this.

In the history of Christian ethical thought different theological emphases have developed often, though by no means always, following confessional traditions. All of these have originated in Europe, and continued there and in the offshoots of European civilization in other parts of the world like the Americas or Australasia. This is the only civilization in which the Christian faith has been so deeply embedded as to mould the structure of society and to make the term "Christendom" an appropriate one. Whether the background was Roman Catholic, Protestant or Orthodox the assumption was broadly the same (though political subjection has for centuries made it more difficult for the Orthodox); people were assumed to be Christian in some significant sense, the institutions of society were assumed to operate on Christian presuppositions, and sins stood out as a precise deviation from a generally accepted norm.

The break-up of this has been frequently analysed. The contemporary discussion of the meaning and Christian significance of secularization is preoccupied with it. There are very few countries where the old Christendom situation persists. Eire may be one.

Two separate questions are now raised for Christian Ethics. What way of behaving should the Church expect of committed Christians? What should Christians wish the State to legislate for the whole community with its mixture of beliefs, agnosticisms and denials? The answers to these questions might be in some instances the same, but the reasons leading to the answer would be different. In most cases the answers will be different.

The first question raises the matter of Church discipline and pastoral care, which has never been an easy one. The question of penal discipline does not often arise now, because in a plural society the offending member simply leaves the fellowship and suffers no social, civil or political disability by so doing. There has been recently, however, the case of Dr Biezanek in the Roman Catholic Church, arising out of her type of contraceptive advice for mothers with large families.[1] But questions of penal discipline would take us too far afield if explored further. Pastoral care is implicit in all that follows, though the confessional may perhaps best be mentioned here. Our Anglican practice of making the ministry of absolution available through the confessional to those whose consciences are unquiet is a valuable one; but in general the confessional is more attuned to situations where sins do stand out as precise deviations, and in general a less formal and more flexible form of pastoral care is required.

The second question presupposes that Christians have a responsibility for life in the world; that they are placed by God's will in structures of family, economic and political life with others of all beliefs and none; that they are in them under God by virtue of their humanity, not by virtue of specifically Christian belief; that it is God's will that they should live and work in the structures to influence them to work justly and humanely, and on a basis which cannot presuppose explicit Christian beliefs. Unless political circumstances make it quite impossible (as in some totalitarian States) Christians are bound to be responsibly involved in the institutions of the plural society in which they live. All this has been much explored in recent years, particularly in the ecumenical movement, and it is assumed in what follows without further explanation or defence.

The importance of keeping these questions distinct can be illustrated from some confusions among Christians in this country in discussing marriage and divorce. What should be expected of Church members is one thing (and there can be more than one opinion about what to do in the case of marriage failures), and what the State should legislate for everyone is another. Formally our State law of marriage enacts the Christian view, but in practice, because the community as a whole does not agree with it sufficiently to hold by it when things go wrong with a marriage, we have a divorce law which amounts to divorce by consent after three years, because those who are determined to part will find ways of proving a matrimonial offence in order to obtain a divorce. Church of England initiatives have recently shown a proper concern for advising the community about a better divorce law as a quite distinct question from that of the Church's own internal discipline,[2] and largely as a result of

---

[1] See *All Things New*, by Anne Biezanek. Peter Smith, 1964.
[2] See *Putting Asunder*, SPCK, 1966.

this a new divorce bill is now before Parliament. Some Christians have expressed doubts on the grounds that it would involve the community in divorce by consent, without realizing that the bill is designed to remedy unsatisfactory features of what may frequently amount to that already, by providing for the dissolution of a marriage only after it has been shown to be already irretrievably wrecked.

All the main approaches to Christian ethics have been thought out in terms of an almost static society, in which the speed of social change was so slow that the next generation could easily carry on from the previous one. All that has changed. There is hardly a country in the world which is not in the midst of rapid social change, and as far as we can foresee it will be a permanent feature of society. Not all theological traditions are equally capable of dealing with this, and all need scrutiny, from this point of view, in a plural society which is ever changing.

If this is the background of the priest's role as a teacher of ethics, his activities have to be considered, first in relation to those who are Church members; secondly in relation to the community at large; though in a mixed society, there will not be a neat division between the two.

Priest and people require a theology which demands precise attention being given to the empirical data of a changing and plural society. This sounds the merest common sense, but in practice most traditional Christian ethical teaching, both Catholic and Protestant, has been too *a priori* in approach. Catholics have interpreted natural law too rigidly and Protestants have interpreted the Bible too rigidly. The current difficulties of the Roman Catholic Church on contraception are an illustration of this.

Empirical data, however, require evaluative criteria in order to assess the significance of alleged facts and the possible consequences of actions. Here it is important that criteria which derive from the Christian understanding of God and man should become articulate. This is particularly urgent in relation to the social sciences. We ought to be able to assume that before ordination Christian doctrine is taught in a way which brings this out, but unfortunately it is not; and we ought to have clergy refresher courses every few years in a man's ministry which takes up these (and other) themes, but there are all too few of them.

The priest's aim within this general theological background is to build each person and each congregation into spiritual maturity in Christ. The Christian life is to be lived boldly in the midst of inevitable uncertainties in making particular decisions, sensitively in relation to others, and flexibly in the ability to learn from experience. There must be awareness of the legitimate range of differences of opinion within the fellowship. The priest's concern will be both with right motivation and the right content of action in particular contexts; both are equally important, and he will guard against the common Protestant tendency to concentrate almost exclusively on motive.

Right motive is nothing less than the mind of Christ being formed in us.

It is an unselfconscious goodness, which cannot be pursued directly but can only arise out of living in the Christian community, taking full advantage of all the means of grace in the fellowship, and losing anxious preoccupations about oneself in seeking and doing God's will in his world. To this end a priest's whole ministry as pastor and liturgical figure is relevant to his concern as a teacher of ethics. Questions of relevant ways of worship and of spirituality for our time arise here but cannot be developed. Certainly it involves making Jesus a real figure, and goodness interesting. One could wish for more help from the New Testament scholars at this point.

To arrive at the right content of action there is no escape from wrestling with the facts, and from the problems which arise from this. The Christian has usually no privileged access to them. Their status may be in dispute. Sometimes desirable facts are unobtainable and decisions wo'n't wait. It is not always clear how far it is relevant to go into further ramifications of the matter. Estimates of probable consequences are uncertain. Apart altogether from personal and social sins which thwart the judgment and impede the practice, there is likely to be a fair range of legitimate differences of opinion among equally sincere Christians. (Some positions are also likely to be seen as untenable.) It is therefore very important to help Christians to distinguish between legitimate and illegitimate differences. Then they will be free to take up all the most thorny problems. Instead, the reverse is usually the case. Church groups shy off contentious subjects for fear that they will "spoil the fellowship". This means that they are pushed on to the margin of many things that matter and it is a disastrous abdication of responsibility. One can see in other countries, for instance Ghana and Nigeria, the fearful weaknesses in the Church to which this leads. Our situation is little better although less dramatically focused.

The Christian walks by faith not by sight. When we see this we are free to raise the "hottest" subjects in Christian discussion and to live with the inevitable disagreements and uncertainties that are our lot. We live as those about whom all is known and has been forgiven in Christ.

How is all this to be achieved? First there is public worship. All worship should be both fixed and contemporary, concerned both with God in Jesus Christ the same yesterday, today and for ever, and at the same time with a particular congregation in a particular context of space and time. Both sermon and prayers are involved here. All preaching is ultimately relevant to ethics, but it is rare to hear sermons on specifically ethical subjects. One can be assured of an attentive hearing for one. Such sermons should arise out of discussion beforehand and allow for discussion afterwards, whether immediately or later in the week. As to prayers, material from the papers, radio and television and local life should be brought in, and laymen frequently associated with them. This cannot be done at the last minute and it requires as much preparation as the sermons.

Then there are the different groups in which Christians can gather, by sex, age, households and occupations. There is a proper place for sheer fellowship and entertainment but not for preoccupation with the trivial. Special groups can be formed across congregations and confessions. A good deal of relevant material is provided from ecumenical and confessional sources. People with relevant experience in the community can be asked to contribute to it. Christians must be alert to the needs of their community. A Church which shuts itself up in its own fellowship will not be listened to, nor does it deserve to be.

In all this the fostering of lay leadership is a main concern of the priest. His job is to make his contribution with others and help where needed. It is not an easy role to play. Few priests are good at leading groups. They talk too much. They cannot bear a silence. They cannot listen to what they consider heresies being uttered without immediately correcting them. The constant expectation that they will "say a few words" has a bad effect on them.

Two further methods of pursuing matters in greater depth are worth mentioning. It may be possible to arrange for a series of extra-mural lectures on ethical subjects, sponsored by the relevant university. This will, of course, only appeal to a minority, and requires a lecturer of sufficient calibre to be sponsored by the university. But they can be extremely valuable, especially as they are always run on the half lecture and half discussion principle and there is, therefore, plenty of give and take between the audience and the lecturer. Another way is for a parish or suitable unit to arrange a conference beginning (for example) with lunch together after Sunday morning church, followed by a talk, discussion in groups, and a concluding session to deal with questions raised, ending about 3.30 p.m. This presupposes reasonable catering facilities. It can be highly successful, involving all ages, from the youth clubs upwards, and diverse occupations.

So far we have been discussing the role of the priest with his own people, or at least other Christians. With the community at large we can be much briefer, not because it is unimporant (quite the contrary), but because the principles are much the same. Their execution is more complicated (because shared presuppositions are less), more time-consuming, and requires even greater flexibility of mind. Here the priest is concerned for good citizenship, for an alive and alert community, for informed participation in affairs, local and national. Out of this concern for the common good will arise the necessary contacts for making a contribution to it. All kinds of societies and *ad hoc* groups, and all kinds of meetings in clubs, pubs, and houses are involved here.

Sometimes different experiences can be focused on a single problem. Not long ago in one area magistrates, solicitors, university dons, social workers, police, medical and psychiatric experts, teachers, parish priests and theologians spent a week-end on the theme of guilt. Such a meeting requires a skilful co-ordinator who can put a good deal of time into its organization and execution. This may be getting beyond what is possible to one parish priest, though not beyond co-ordinated effort.

Behind these types of activity and issuing from some of them may well be what have been rather confusingly called "middle axioms". These are conclusions as to the general direction which Christians should press in some area of ethical decision. They arise out of a Christian judgement brought alongside the empirical data of the issue involved. They are an attempt to evaluate trends, to indicate the general ends to work for at a particular time, without prescribing a detailed route. Situations may be so tangled that no consensus arises. If one does, it comes out of relevant experience. Not all who contribute need be Christians, but the priest should be one who contributes. The consensus may be wrong (empirical judgments are inescapably uncertain), but it will have a good deal of informal authority, and the onus will lie on those who disagree to establish their case. If such "axioms" can be arrived at they give something relevant to say, and help to bridge the gulf between Christian and non-Christian (and between cleric and layman). Much of the material from ecumenical conferences lies in this middle ground; more attention should be paid to it as a basis for tackling local situations. Industry, commerce, social welfare, race relations are obvious areas to think of in this connexion.

In all this there is immense scope; but much hard work is needed, much casting of bread upon the waters, much ability to listen to others, much mediating of the views of one person to another who hardly ever meet and don't find it easy to understand one another's language and style of approach. It requires the spiritual resources to live with a lot of untidy and unresolved problems. The priest is in an excellent position to do this. He will almost always be accepted as an "honest broker" if he goes about it the right way, that is to say with tact and free from any strain of triumphalism.

Four things may be said in conclusion.

The priest should hold fast to Christ as the source and goal of his understanding.

The priest should not always want to have something different to say *qua* Christian from what some others may be saying. Fortunately in our pluralist society ethical attitudes and moral decisions often overlap. Christians may find themselves in agreement with others. (Of course, they may not.) The desire always to be different was the undoing of the old Christendom group.

The priest should therefore welcome allies where he can find them. In this country many humanists go along with Christians. This is a matter for rejoicing, not for worry lest the faith be contaminated. Equally it is necessary to show where humanism can end by being inhuman in the light of a deeper humanism in Christ.

The priest should encourage action as well as talk. Each needs to feed the other. Where possible the action should be community based rather than Church based; and where a Church basis is appropriate it should, wherever possible, be ecumenically based. There is a lot to be done before the Churches habitually act like this; but this is what it means to take a plural society seriously.

8

Clergymen and their Bishops

ALAN WEBSTER

When the Editor of THEOLOGY posed the question "What sort of relation ought to exist between a clergyman and his diocesan bishop, suffragan bishop, archdeacon, etc.?" I first thought of particular bishops I had known both before and after becoming a clergyman. Dr Francis Luke Paget of Chester confirmed with the clear conviction that there was a moment of supreme importance in one's service of God; I remembered being told that when his car was overturned in an accident he felt no embarrassment or pious affectation at kneeling in the road with the workmen who rescued him and simply thanking God. Dr Williams of Carlisle, with a burglar's face and a scholar's mind, cared enough about ordinands to make them think for themselves and to shake them out of prejudices. Dr Leslie Hunter's ordinations in the blitzed city of Sheffield spoke strongly of the Church's eternal mission and the need for faith and courage to fulfil it. One of those ordained beside me was a German refugee pastor, rescued by the Bishop of Chichester, a quiet reminder that the office of a bishop extends outside his diocese and has obligations not to be quenched by wartime clamour. I thought, too, of my institution as incumbent in a dour Norman church by the then Bishop of Durham, crowded with men and women, who seemed to expect so much of their parish. For most clergymen this is the essence of the bishop's office – the responsible leadership of the Church of God. All the bishops I have mentioned were responsible men, taking responsible decisions and calling on God to bless their work.

The bishop is invested with authority and in appropriate occasions with discretionary responsibility to decide what is best. He must work with his colleagues and with the Church, clerical and lay; but there will be moments of loneliness in his work, as there certainly were for the Bishop of Chichester. Naturally in his work he will guide rather than order and trust rather than interfere.

The formula often used at institutions, "My cure and thine" is unfortunate if understood as suggesting that other clergy are the delegates of bishops.[1] Not only have parishes a vitality and responsibility of their own, but all Christians are in the first place answerable to God and accountable to him, and no theory of obedience in the Christian Church should try to evade this, or indeed can, as Charles Davis has demonstrated in his *A Question of Conscience*. The idea of popes, bishops, presbyteries, professors or conferences having an absolute claim to obedience ought never to have arisen. Even St Ignatius of Antioch was primarily concerned to encourage harmony in churches with bishops, presbyters and deacons all determined to do the will of God, not to establish a dictatorship of monarchical bishops.

When the bishop has a clear and defined role as in Confirmation, the closer the co-operation the better he does his work. Before a recent school confirmation the headmaster, other masters concerned, and the chaplain, spent twenty-four hours away from the school discussing confirmation and afterwards the chaplain and the bishop considered their findings. The bishop at the confirmation gave magnificent addresses, both to those being confirmed and to the parents, and behaved with the quiet, knowledgeable confidence of someone inside the community he was leading. His authority was increased not diminished by the careful consultation; the feeling that he was "with it" in no way detracted from the sense of fatherly wisdom he brought to an occasion which may decline into a conventional affair half way between O and A levels.

The relations between bishops and clergymen have had their ups and downs in the past hundred years. Perhaps the nadir was in 1876 when Bishop Fraser of Manchester did not prevent the prosecution for ritualism of S. F. Green, vicar of Miles Platting; S. F. Green spent more than a year in Lancaster gaol. Recently there have been cases of heavy-handed treatment when it would have been wiser to trust responsible men on the spot; here ecumenical relations, industrial mission and inter-faith services have been the occasion of some timid prohibitions. Authorities who forbid inter-faith services, even on Commonwealth Day, should first experience the inter-faith dialogues of some of the Ashrams or the inter-faith public services attended by Church leaders of different denominations in India. Bishops, like priests, serve in the Church of God, a body which extends far outside England, and has a duty to proclaim the gospel courageously to many cultures. But these are unusual incidents; the exponents of the "New Theology" have been met on the whole with reasoned discussion

---

[1] Even "Confer a share in the bishop's cure of souls" (*Partners in Ministry*, CIO, 1967, p. 54) is a questionable phrase.

not with ex-communication. As the Lord is the way, the truth and the light, it is, as Bishop Kirk used to teach, sound moral practice and not pietistic sentimentality to hold by the maxim "Great is the truth and it shall prevail".

The clergymen's resistance to the guidance of diocesan bishops has also had its ups and downs. The nadir here is the occasion when the Parson's Freehold is supported in order to maintain the gap between what Dr. L. S. Hunter has called "the legal minimum and the vocational minimum".[1] It would do us all good at times to be asked for a worksheet showing what we have done in the past week. But today the failures of clergymen are less due to laziness or professional incompetence than to the absence of occasions when there can be hard study and careful thought about the purpose of God for his Church today – and actual pastoral work together based on common decisions. Directions from above are ineffective. Suffragan bishops and archdeacons cannot usefully give charges when many of those being "charged" are more experienced or more learned; but they could help towards changes of attitude and thinking by working alongside other clergymen. The suffragan bishop or archdeacon who is also vicar of a large parish (as in some Lancashire dioceses) has better lines of communication because he can be seen to be doing a vital task and doing it well.

The key to better relations is much more delegation so that bishops can give more time to leadership based on rational persuasion. Some dioceses should be smaller, but all could be happier if there were clearer definitions of function.[2] Vague responsibility tends to actual irresponsibility with the disastrous results seen in many dioceses–huge parishes without curates in the most difficult areas. The familiar scene at diocesan conferences of bishops with their staff looking down from the platform with an expression of friendly but baffled puzzlement is a symptom of the disease. The audience sitting row after row can almost hear the platform murmur: "Why do they stand for the Parson's Freehold?" "Why do they oppose the amalgamation of parishes and the demolition of redundant churches?" "Why can't they see we must raise the quota for the salary for another youth chaplain?" "This diocese is one big happy family and this opposition has got to stop."

Professor Bernard Crick's Gaitskell Memorial lecture for 1968[3] deals

---

[1] See L. S. Hunter "Professional Standards in the Ministry", *Crucible*, Oct. 1963, pp. 109–15.

[2] Putting episcopacy into commission and setting up many Church Assembly committees is a dubious remedy. "The Church Assembly proliferates councils and committees. It needs to practice birth control. The weakness spreads to the dioceses. Something must be done, it is said, and instead of following a good precedent and responding 'Whom shall we send?' or 'Who will go?', a committee is appointed." *The Church of England*, ed. L. S. Hunter (Penguin, 1966, p. 76).

[3] Summarized in *New Society*, 25 Jan. 1968, p. 115.

with the parallel situation in our political malaise – that citizens feel that they are treated like children and not told. Dr Crick writes

> Public explanation is no abstract mystery or new heresy. The British army, even, chastened by defeat in 1940, came round to explaining. Soldiers were actually told and briefed, in some sort of manner, about the objects and tactics of local and even major actions.

The whole of Dr Crick's thesis is relevant, but his plea for openness and carrying people with them willingly and comprehendingly should appeal to all members of the Church of England. Now that the Church is committed simultaneously to a reform of its government, its law, its liturgy, its administration, its clerical training programme, and its relations with other churches, there will be no effective government unless the bishops find time to confer together and with their dioceses. The bishops must decide on *priorities* for themselves and their dioceses if this immense programme is to be carried through without halting the pastoral and educational work of the church, and must be prepared to discuss with clergy and lay people the reasons for their priorities.

The need to concentrate on essentials is the upshot of much recent research on the doctrine of episcopacy. The late Dr Telfer's discussion of *The Office of a Bishop*, while stressing the essential functions of the bishop of deciding what is for the good of the Church and examining his role as making the final decisions about ordination, acting with his colleagues as a judge of theological issues, as a magistrate, a guardian of the faith and as a trustee, does not hesitate to describe the later doctrine of the apostolic succession as a historical myth created by Latin churchmen.[1] Dr Telfer encourages us to distinguish between historical claims which research does not justify and the values which were and are at stake. As the doctrine of episcopacy is being stripped of doubtful historical claims, and the making and enthroning of a bishop of oddly misleading ritual – battering on the cathedral door as if he was an outsider – so this demythologizing process ought to make it easier for bishops to strip their days of many trivial tasks.

A significant change is taking place in some dioceses in the relation between the bishop and the junior clergy. Though some bishops do not meet their candidates until the ordination retreat, almost all give sufficient time to this retreat itself, staying with the candidates, or if the numbers are small, having them to stay, to establish a meeting of minds. The perfunctory impersonal pre-ordination meetings of the nineteenth century typified by Dr E. H. Browne, Bishop of Ely, whose contact with ordinand fellows was dinner on the eve of ordination at 5 p.m., a reminder to be in the cathedral at 10 o'clock in the morning, and a sugges-

---

[1] Ibid., p. 119 (Darton Longman and Todd, 1962). See also *The Historic Episcopate*, ed. K. M. Carey (Dacre Press, 1954) and E. Schlink *The Coming Christ and The Coming Church* (Oliver and Boyd, 1967), p. 232.

tion to ring for the butler if they needed port, have been replaced by pre-ordination "retreats" at which bishop and ordinands begin to understand each other. When the generation gap is so fatally wide, to listen may be as important as to deliver a charge. A recent enquiry among 100 men ordained in the last ten years showed that the great majority of these men felt that their relationship with their ordaining bishop was close and valuable, whereas the sly shade of the rural dean, or even of the archdeacon or suffragan was very much in the background. Much is said of the "family of the diocese" or reviving the rural deaneries but some of these members of the bishop's staff appear to have neither time nor inclination to be on terms of personal friendship with recent arrivals. Many bishops however do succeed here.

The nexus between those exercising *episcope* and the rest of the Church has several strands, but friendship should be one of the strongest. Obedience to authority will not hold by itself. Vatican II, while stating that bishops have the sacred right and the duty before the Lord to make laws for their subjects, to pass judgment on them and to moderate everything pertaining to the ordering of worship and the apostolate, urges them to regard the priests, who are their co-workers, as sons and friends, and bids both bishops and priests to acknowledge the just freedom which belongs to the laity.[1]

Without trust the relationship between clergy and bishops and other controlling authorities can become sour. Charles Davis has spoken of the "desperate loneliness" of some Roman Catholics, and of Roman Catholic structures as destructive of genuine human relationships. Dr Kai Baago, the distinguished Danish historian, is leaving the ministry of the Lutheran Church of Denmark after working in Asia because he finds it "incredible that Jesus should ever have intended any such organization with paid clergy and pastoral committees, with synods and elections".[2] That relationships within the Church should be personal rather than those of rulers or magistrates or business executives is becoming vital, not only to the survival of institutional churches but to the understanding of Christianity itself.

To establish a discipline which is not a discipline of financial, legal or administrative coercion – these are what the Gentiles seek after – means that the ministry must experience the kind of trust which exists between friends.[3] At present this exists only in part. This trust links the bishop and those he ordains; it links an archdeacon who helps a hard-pressed curate during an interregnum; it links an elderly vicar who really tries to understand the radical curate who, perhaps like William Temple at the time of his ordination, suspends judgment about the Virgin Birth; it links the

[1] The Decree on the Church.
[2] Dr Kai Baago "Honestly Speaking" in *The United Church Review*, July 1967, p. 149.
[3] See P. Baelz "Obedience" in THEOLOGY, 1963, pp. 185–89.

clergyman who does what he is asked to do, even if he does not wholly agree with the bishop whose vision he does not yet share. Trust does not depend on intimate personal knowledge, nor does it require that every diocese should be tiny, or that vicars and curates must be of the same generation and in full theological accord. Trust takes time to grow, but without it all the reforming reports from the Church Assembly and Tufton Street will be paper exercises. Vision and competence earn trust.

Considerable strain on relationships within the ministry is caused by both bishops and clergy who have failed to grasp the degree of theological comprehensiveness inevitable in the Church today, and find it hard to trust and to work with those with whom they disagree. Hensley Henson was a telling witness. He suffered greatly from the unjustified attacks of Bishop Gore and the English Church Union; Gore actually going so far as to say "I think we ought not to accept him as a brother bishop". Reflecting on the way his episcopal brethren treated him, Henson felt "a bleak sense of isolation".[1] There are dioceses today where relationships are made difficult by a party attitude, so that clergymen whose only fault is to admire the Bishop of Woolwich or Dr Mascall or Dr Packer feel "a bleak sense of isolation". That stalwart north-county eighteenth-century bishop, William Nicholson, was once amused to discover in a Lutheran church a window containing the figures of the Devil, Ignatius Loyola and John Calvin, under which was the caption "The three greatest enemies of Christ and the Christian religion".[2] Some in England, I fear, behave as if they could identify the three Anglican doctors whom I have named earlier; surely modern Anglican bishops and clergy and laymen in both provinces should be sufficiently robust to rejoice in the varieties of the theologians, even when expounded and occasionally misunderstood by enthusiastic disciples.

Despite these strains the enquiry already mentioned revealed much greater trust within the ministry than pessimists allow. Of the 100 men, 76 had had an easy relationship with their first vicar, only 21 a difficult one. Nor were their friendships narrowly clerical. Asked to whom they would find it easiest to talk about the things that mattered most they answered: lay people associated with the Church (77); lay people not associated with the Church (66); vicar (51); the bishop (41); the rural dean (30). A number naturally suggested "one's fellow curates".

In the same enquiry an attempt was made to compare relationships inside and outside the Church, and again the replies were encouraging. Sixty-four men had been in employment before ordination, and in answer to questions about relationships (the questions were asked in a three category list: 1. those responsible for them; 2. among equals; and 3. among those for whom they had responsibility) 30, 24 and 34 thought

[1] See N. Sykes, THEOLOGY, Oct. 1942, p. 197.
[2] F. G. James, North Country Bishop (Yale, 1956, p. 11).

relationships better in the Church; 24, 33 and 25 thought them much the same: and 12, 11 and 4 thought them worse in the Church than in their previous employment. The relationships which involved policy-making were less satisfactory. Ninety-four thought they had had a fair share in shaping policy in their parishes, but only 27 felt satisfied at diocesan level. Deanery meetings were also frustrating. Only 21 found them sources of information; only 19 places where decisions are made: whereas 84 and 86 replied "no" to these two questions. Neither deanery nor diocesan conferences appear to be effective as points where consultation and explanation can take place, whereas experiments in parishes are being carried out. To the question "Have you seen hopeful changes since the time of your ordination, carried out or obstructed at parish, deanery and diocesan level?", 83, 50 and 41, believed they had seen hopeful changes at these three levels (11, 48 and 51 had not), and 57, 35 and 44 had seen hopeful changes obstructed (where 41, 53 and 45 had not). Seventy-seven held the view that the "New Theology" had been helpful in their personal work (10 not). Thirty-seven believed that it had also helped in parishes (11 not), but 43 felt that it had not yet reached parish level. Friendships are clearly leaping denominational barriers; 94 are on terms of personal friendship with Free Church ministers (87 with Methodists, 41 with Congregationalists, 39 with Baptists, 28 with Presbyterians), 70 with Roman Catholic priests and 70 with humanists.

This enquiry points to reasonable personal relationships between diocesan bishops and younger clergy, but relative failure in relationship at other levels. The old assumptions that "archdeacons, etc." could be effective simply because of their official position no longer holds, and some dioceses are combining the archdeaconries and suffragan bishop's areas. The development of the view that all those in authority, including bishops, are to be the pastors and friends of the clergy is taking time. Episcopacy survived in England partly because it was politically essential for the Tudors and early Stuarts ("No bishop, no King") just as Presbyterianism took root in Scotland partly for political reasons. Bishops in England have rarely been popular heroes even with the clergy – apart from the three martyred at Oxford or the seven imprisoned in the Tower. In the nineteenth and early twentieth centuries bishops again became embroiled with some of their clergy over evangelicalism, ritualism and modernism, and prelacy only died yesterday. More experience of episcopacy outside England, especially in Scotland and the Church of South India, is needed if this new working relationship is to become effective.

But if the bishop is to be treated as "a person to whom is entrusted . . . discretion to decide in appropriate situations what course is for the good of the Church, and tends to the fulfilment of God's purpose"[1] or as being a pastor empowered and authorized to look after the community with the

---

[1] W. Telfer, *The Office of a Bishop*, p. vii.

solicitude of the Father whom Jesus Christ reveals,[1] we need to give bishops the encouragement to be courageous. We must also give them more freedom to think so that they can be more ready both to teach and to lead. Must a diocesan or a suffragan chair so many committees and even sub-committees in London or the provinces? The Church is fortunate in its laymen and women – and surely too in many of its inferior clergy. Relationships within the ministry weaken when episcopal chairmen, overworked by incessant meetings, cannot give thought to the long-term planning which the revolution in English life demands. The changes in English life (not least in education, a traditional Christian concern) are both exciting and fundamental; guidance in priorities and a Christian understanding of what things are most worth doing are what the Church expects from "bishops, archdeacons, etc." If the Church insists on smothering its bishops in typescript, expecting them to chair committees (suffragans the sub-committees), and treating them as easily shocked and so to be protected from knowing what is actually happening, then the Church would do far better with a Presbyterian or Conference system of government, and relations within the ministry would be much more straightforward. "Just go ahead and do it but don't tell me", a remark sometimes made in answer to a request for advice on a fresh initiative, is more acceptable than a negative; but bishops exist to give help in discretionary questions and ought to be prepared to share responsibility for what is new.

There are dangers in the present drive for reform which could divide the ministry. If bishops and their advisers give priority to London committees they will become not only inaccessible but without influence, like admirals without a navy. The General Synod, possibly of 543 persons, may sit for as many as twenty days each year[2] and the Morley Report's suggestion of ministry commissions will demand even more time from the higher clergy. Ought the Church to determine to keep episcopacy in its system, i.e. in the dioceses, and allow it to work? A bishop who has spent years in his home cities, knows the people, including those who may not go to church but still respect much of the Church's work, may well be better able than commissions to fill vacant livings if he consults adequately – and his decisions will be respected. Episcopacy expects much from bishops, and those who commend it to other churches ought to have the courage of their convictions and actually use it. It has the great merit of emphasizing personal responsibility, accountability, and initiative. There must be reforms; the haphazardness of appointments, the extraordinary length of some vacancies, and the casualness of the handover, both of dioceses and parishes, suggest that the Church is still a lumbering eighteenth-century stage coach. The solution is not

[1] L. S. Hunter, *The English Church*, p. 70.
[2] See *Crucible*, Sept. 1967, p. 144.

more committees but more decisions based on a comprehensible, understood policy.

The administration of religion is apt to lead those who write about it as
well as those who are involved in its techniques far from the New Testament and the Servant Church, which the ministry is concerned to streng-
then. The Church is the one historic human institution based on the
conviction that God has revealed in the Gospel the meaning of life and
the Church is to "wait" on the human family to remind it of this fact.
This is the core of the work of the ministry. It is not sentimentality to
suggest that when the ministry does this convinced "waiting", it is united.
Those bishops who have brought the office alive here, as well as others
seen at work overseas, such as Lesslie Newbigin, Bishop in Madras
(has the time come for English bishops to use the humbler and more
realistic "in" instead of "of"?) command respect because they serve.
The great priests of our century, T. W. Pym, B. K. Cunningham, Peter
Green, Hugh Lister, like many other unsung of the inferior clergy,
could never have served as they did except in a Church which saw freedom and trust as vital to all relationships which look for inspiration to
Jesus Christ.

9

Head and Members
The Priest and the Community
he Serves

HELEN OPPENHEIMER

The problem is nothing less than the nature of the Body of Christ. Are Christians expressing, constituting, or laying hold of a genuine reality when they partake in the life of the local church, whether at the altar, over the coffee cups, at the Parochial Church Council, or turning towards the outer world? What is the role of the priest in relation to that reality?

It may well seem that his task is to straddle, like an involuntary Colossus, a deep and perhaps widening crevasse between theology and everyday life. The existence of this rift can be indicated, though possibly rather unfairly, by pointing out for example that L. S. Thornton's great theological book *The Common Life in the Body of Christ* is evidently not about "common life" as anyone in fact lives it. From the other side the sinister character of the rift may be seen by considering the growth of the expression "But that's theology" as a way of cutting short purely abstract and useless theorizing whatever the subject matter.[1]

There is a most urgent need for a bridge over the crevasse, an applied theology of the Body of Christ; and if this theology is going to turn out to be much too difficult for the ordinary Christian to understand, then it must be said that there is something wrong with it. Of course it may be a deep mystery which one is not yet holy enough to enter into, but that is another matter from sheer intellectual abstruseness. No doubt there are *also* great stretches of Christian theology which just are abstruse as well

[1] E.g. H. J. Blackham, *Religion in a Modern Society*, p. 154.

as mysterious: would we not expect the doctrines of the Trinity and the Incarnation to be beyond our intelligence?[1] Nothing forbids us to study intellectually the science of God, but nothing guarantees that we shall get very far, for we may well suppose that God is infinitely clever as well as infinitely holy, and can lead his own life without our comprehension. But such doctrines as the Church and the Atonement should surely not take human understanding out of its depth so quickly. If they are true they must be capable of emerging into the experience of the ordinary Christian, not in so far as he is intelligent but in so far as he is becoming holy. If these doctrines are beyond most of us, it is as if the applied sciences of cooking or bringing up children were beyond the ordinary woman. Ought a book about the Body of Christ, then, to enlighten a vicar on how to run his parish? In general the answer must be Yes, for the same reason as the answer to the converse question, Ought a PCC to discuss theology? must be Yes. The Body of Christ, when it becomes specific, *is* the local church; the agenda of the PCC, whether or not this is realized, *is* theology.

Another way of saying the same thing is that the theology and sociology of the Church cannot be taken apart. L. S. Thornton contrasts[2] the concept of the Church as a "sociological entity" with the theological concept of a "single divine–human organism reaching from heaven to earth", but the contrast is surely false. In so far as the "divine–human organism" is a reality it is bound to manifest itself *as* a "sociological entity", just as the body of Christ Incarnate was manifested as a physical entity.

To emphasize that the Church is "more" than a sociological entity sounds well but has risks: the same sort of risks as in emphasizing that God is "more" than personal. The negative picture defeats the positive and one is left with a conception too rarified to find ready application. At the present juncture it seems more constructive to pull the theology and the sociology together as closely as possible, not to let them slip further apart.[3] Let it even be affirmed that the doctrine of the Church as the Body of Christ if it were fully realized would turn out to be, so to speak, the sociology of heaven. That heaven could have a sociology should not be a more shocking supposition than that earth could have a theology: perhaps indeed the two suppositions are the same.

The epistles of St Paul may be called in evidence here. The tendency of the Apostle to weave together high speculation about the Body of Christ with seemingly prosaic administrative arrangements, with the interchange of social goodwill and with practical moral exhortation,

---

[1] As C. S. Lewis put it, Christianity if true is "bound to be difficult – at least as difficult as modern Physics, and for the same reason" (*Mere Christianity*, p. 123).

[2] Page 2.

[3] Here I am differing in emphasis, though I hope not in substance, from the Editor in his article (above p.3). See also K. L. Schmidt, *Bible Keywords*, The Church, p.21.

might not in itself provide a precedent for the future conduct of Church affairs. We might after all conceive ourselves to have developed our thinking and drawn useful distinctions which in early days were only implicit. But the authority and liveliness, adding up to a kind of inescapable authenticity, in St Paul's procedure of weaving the strands together, compared with the deadness and limpness of our own tendency to draw them apart, surely gives one to think.[1] When he shoots from one live metaphor to another and brings them to bear upon Christian living, do we really want to turn metaphor into technicality and then insulate the resulting theory from contact with practical affairs?

The next temptation is for this Pauline authenticity to lose itself in glibness. In reaction against making technicalities of the great metaphors of the Church it is fatally easy to make slogans of them. There is a fashionable line of thought each step of which is attractive but which skims along the surface of great matters, arriving so quickly and easily at its destination that not much is gathered on the way. We are the Body of Christ and severally members thereof, and this means us, in ordinary parish life. This seems a simple method of exorcizing the false individualism whose church services were "inward-looking" and whose service to the world was self-righteous and probably paternalistic. In fellowship with one another we can "be the Church" and this fellowship will automatically supply the needed link between "religion" and "the world". Now we can patronize Bishop Butler for his cautious reminder to his congregation that the early Christians "almost literally esteemed themselves as members one of another".[2]

The keyword is "fellowship" so the test must be its quality. Is it not quite apparent that the friendliness, politeness and goodwill which flourishes agreeably in innumerable parishes today simply will not bear the weight which this arugment puts upon it? To confuse an inferior substitute with the fellowship of the Holy Ghost may not be to commit the sin against him which cannot be forgiven, but it is surely to take his name in vain. If Brunner[3] is right that

> the church is the true community, the community founded upon God's love. It is the only community that is not built upon an egocentric motive

we must simply say "Heaven help us"; or take such an extremely Protesttant view of the Church as to allow for its total invisibility and discounthe visible Church almost entirely.

What has gone wrong? It is not that people today are incapable of deep

---

[1] I should hate to suggest that all modern theology of the Church is dead and limp. A most exciting exception is C. H. Dodd's article on "The Communion of Saints" in his *New Testament Studies*. (I should also like to acknowledge a debt to E. Best, *One Body in Christ*, for his constructive emphasis on the metaphorical character of St Paul's thinking.)

[2] Rolls Chapel Sermons. I: I.   [3] *I believe in the living God*, p. 136.

relationships, but that by and large they are not finding them in the context of Church life. Not only are many sensitive and high-minded people entirely outside the Church: loyal and whole-hearted Christians may be loyal but by no means whole-hearted parishioners. Their centre of gravity lies elsewhere.

The recognition of the prevalence of the virtuous outsider could prove a red herring here. A kind of sociological over-simplification imposes a false pattern upon the problems of Christian community. If "Christian nation" has indeed given place to "plural society", does this not make the Church simply a missionary Church again? But then why does our Church life not seem to have anything like the quality which the Church life of the early Christians evidently had? Anxious Christians begin to wonder whether the Church really is dying at last? One cannot help taking unhappily to heart some words of F. D. Maurice,

> It would be the utter uprooting of our faith if we found that there was no such body as the apostle told us there should be.[1]

Hereupon a rather desperate exercise of will-power is apt to be put in hand, with Church people both clerical and lay trying to whip themselves up into the sort of completeness of community feeling which they read of in the New Testament. The upshot of such attempts to "make Christian ellowship real" is likely to be either well-meaning insincerity or discouragement or a kind of uneasy blend of the two, while all the time the sheer complexity of our present Church situation is underestimated. When a single individual can be within himself a kind of microcosm of a plural society, it is bound to be the case that neither "national Church" nor "mission Church" is a sufficiently elaborate description of where we are now and of the relationships in which Christians find themselves involved. It follows that there is no presumption that the kinds of fellowship natural to either folk religion or to a company of missionaries will be straightforwardly applicable to ourselves. In this connexion, an interesting article by Barbara Wollaston in a recent number of *Parish and People*[2] casts wholesome doubt on unreasonable expectations of "fellowship" and community participation in developing urban neighbourhoods. Enthusiastic involvement, she suggests,

> on the part of new area residents may be as much a neurotic symptom as is the doctor's surgery filled by people with very minor ailments. The decline in participation as the years pass by may mean that the community is settling down.[3]

To ignore such facts is "to work with a built-in factor of discouragement".[4] The application of these considerations to the affairs of many parishes is sufficiently apparent.

[1] *Theological Essays*, p. 276.
[2] "Urban Neighbourhoods Today", *Parish and People*, Autumn 1967.
[3] Page 7.   [4] Page 11.

Up to a point this argument has been in line with the current insistence on secularization. Church people are continually being urged to get away from "religion" in the sense of dutiful involvement in Church affairs and to hallow their real worldly relationships. But contrariwise, the "religionless Christianity" people are also vulnerable here. When they say "get away from religion" in the sense of dogma and ritual and leave only Christian fellowship as the essential nature of the Church, they are thoroughly committed to the effective quality of that fellowship as their only standing-ground.

A short way with these anxieties is apt to be proposed here. Perhaps the whole difficulty comes from being too subjective. In the Christian life it is not deep and subtle relationships which matter but a simple, though of course costly, orientation of the will. The *agape* on which Christian fellowship is based is nothing to do with feelings but with turning towards one's neighbour, any neighbour, and treating him as the child of God, as a Thou and not an It. To such exhortations we are all accustomed and heaven forbid that we should repudiate the insights they summarize. But to stop short at this stage is almost inevitably to set forth Christian fellowship as a matter of quantity of relationships rather than quality, to eliminate selfishness not by positive enlargement of capacity for love, but by loss of depth. A great deal that is written and said today about community, I–Thou relationships and the love of the neighbour seems dangerously to ignore the magnificent multiplicity and intricacy of the ways in which human beings can enter into relationship with one another.[1]

Of course the good Samaritan, the man who sees humanity even in the potentially alien or repulsive, and who acts on this perception at considerable trouble to himself, is a key Christian figure. Perhaps he was late home to his own Samaritan family for the sake of this stranger. One might call him a model example of seeing the essentials of a situation, of getting his priorities right, and by his true neighbourliness he showed up some false "neighbours". But he is not thereby a pattern for every kind of Christian relationship; and in particular, for the fellowship of the Body of Christ he is a pattern only in a negative way. There is nothing to suggest that he went about looking for strangers to be kind to in preference to entering into more profound relationships, nor that he would have been a very well-integrated Samaritan if he had. There could be stages in Church history when the members of Christ's body would do well to take more note of the Johannine figures of Lazarus and his sisters or the beloved disciple, at least to the extent of learning that the Lord was evidently not afraid of or hostile towards specific relationships, however urgently he warned his followers against selfish exclusiveness.

---

[1] For an admirable corrective to this tendency, see Harvey Cox, *The Secular City*, pp. 40–49.

Why then should one suppose that the Church is at present in such a stage, and that the perpetual dangers of false emphasis are not being incorrectly located? Many examples could be given: trivial examples admittedly, but inevitably so when the malady being diagnosed is a form of chronic triviality.

For instance, there are several prevalent forms of misunderstanding between clergy and people which surely spring from a fundamental unreality in actual Christian fellowship. The normal reaction of parishioners to a new way of doing things which they do not find congenial is not to approach the vicar to explain their objections or find out what the changes mean: they silently and with a deadly politeness stay away from the services. This would hardly be the initial reaction of the members of a family whose mother failed to supply them with suitable meals.

A similar lack of communication is apt to occur over infant baptism. Of course "public baptism of infants" means what it says, and of course a large part of the significance of the rite is the making the child a member of the Christian Church. But in our mobile society the chances are not high that a particular person will lead much of his life in the particular Christian community in which he happens to be born and baptized. To the child's parents, deeply concerned with their new baby's welfare, the real community to which they and their baby belong is the large or small group of relations and friends who will still be theirs wherever fortune takes them to live. If an artificial concourse of benevolent neighbours however Christian is proposed as a substitute for those most nearly concerned in witnessing the ceremony of making their child a member of Christ they will sense a falsehood, even if they are unable to put this awareness into words. A parish baptism which it is impossible for grandparents, aunts and uncles from elsewhere to attend can represent as sharp a cleavage of theology from life as an exclusive Saturday christening hidden from the public gaze.

All this matters, because what is happening is that the vocabulary of fellowship is being debased. It is distressing to find in a book about a parish church, in the midst of much wisdom, the words "an unfriendly, unsociable Christian is a contradiction in terms".[1] One sees what is meant, but misunderstanding can result. A man may not be gregarious because, for instance, he is acutely shy, seriously overworked, recently bereaved, or seldom in one place for long, and such reasons do not necessarily impair his Christian faith. A patronal festival may be hopefully described as a great occasion, but it is a rare patronal festival which rouses or should arouse such keen enjoyment as a human birthday party. It makes a poor thing of the Body of Christ to blur such differences and to seem to reduce it to such inessential manifestations. Particularly if heaven itself is to be

[1] M. Hocking, *The Parish Seeks the Way*, p. 23.

interpreted in terms of personal relationships with God and one another,[1] it is imperative not to have an impoverished understanding of what a personal relationship can be. It is therefore necessary to insist that the kind of fellowship which can be scheduled to happen in parish halls is not better or more authentic than the kind which spontaneously occurs on a family outing or between friends discussing far into the night, or colleagues working hard to get something done. Any of these might be doors into or distractions from the kingdom of heaven.

What the Church urgently needs at the present time is a theology of friendship. As long as "fellowship" is treated on the one hand as a sort of watered-down friendship and on the other hand is simultaneously set up as superior to the real thing, the vigour of the Body of Christ is bound to be impaired. The trouble spreads well beyond Church circles, and the word "friend" is itself becoming similarly debased. One hears of people who become "prisoners' friends", no doubt doing admirable liaison work between those in prison and the outer world, but who are sensibly advised not to reveal their own telephone numbers for fear of impingement upon their private lives. Likewise the task of the Samaritans is to "befriend", in necessary distinction from the somewhat different rôle of the professionals in these social fields; but when a human being is set on his feet again his friend moves on to the next person who needs him. A much more sensitive and perhaps intricate apparatus of words and ideas is needed to allow us to do justice to the true complications and subtleties of such relationships.[2] At the same time those who simply are friends in the basic meaning of the word have no need to try to assimilate their relationship precisely to any of these helping roles. There is truth which is sometimes overlooked in a German *Spruch*:[3]

> "Freund in der Not" will nicht viel heissen;
> Hilfreich möchte sich mancher erweisen,
> Aber die neidlos ein Glück dir gönnen,
> Die darfst du warhlich "Freunde" nennen.

But still the object of the exercise should not be to glorify friendship or any other deep human relationship as simply self-justifying or an end in itself. One would have to reckon not only with "I have called you

---

[1] I have tried to suggest such an interpretation in *The Character of Christian Morality*, pp. 75–76.

[2] Cf. Dorothy Emmet, *Rules, Roles and Relations*, Chapter VIII "Persons and Personae"; e.g. p. 169.

[3] It is by, I think, Heyse: I noted it down from an anthology a quarter of a century ago and have not been able to check it further. The translation is roughly as follows:

> Friend in need will not signify much;
> Many would like to show themselves full of helpfulness.
> But those who unenvying do not grudge thee a happiness
> These thou darest truly call friends.

friends",[1] but with "If ye love them which love you, what reward have ye? do not even the publicans the same?"[2] There is scant comfort in the New Testament for those who confine their love to one small circle however dear. The present plea is not for a headlong flight from public civilities to private affections, but for a refusal to substitute either for the other, an appreciation of the range and depth of human capacities for love and goodwill, an exploration of the potentialities of personal relationships in Christian understanding.

Meantime, what is the parish priest supposed to be doing? If all his efforts to foster goodwill and neighbourliness are to be seen as peripheral, is he simply left as a sort of witch-doctor, with no distinctive role but that of dispenser of sacraments in some magical sense? It is worth pointing out that even this, adequately understood, could be much. If the sacraments are in any real sense means of grace they have somehow to be made available in the sense of locatable, and this is not magic but common-sense. Whatever "apostolic succession" means it must surely amount to at least this, that the Christian Church is findable; and it is through identifiable human beings that this comes about. The nature of the continuity is regrettably at issue, but it cannot but be through particular people that we are assured of belonging to the same Body as the Apostles. Granted this, it would be faithless not to suppose that such availability is used by the Holy Spirit for the building up of the Body of Christ. This line of thought is borne out by the fact that where one's Church is most simply used as a facility, as for instance away from home and especially in foreign chaplaincies, one is often most vividly aware of it as a fellowship of Christians.

But this need not be all. Many parish clergymen could surely take heart rather than discouragement from that Collect asking God's grace for the clergy and congregations which is emphatically addressed to him "who alone workest great marvels". It can be invigorating to see Christian fellowship as a great marvel, neither to be presumed upon nor on the other hand anxiously cultivated. True Christian fellowship may well turn out to be something like happiness or originality, lost as soon as it is directly sought but flourishing strongly as soon as self-conscious attention is removed from it. If a parish devotes itself to providing for real needs, worship primarily because that is what it is constituted to do, instruction when people are ignorant, sociability when they are lonely, fund-raising when money is needed, social service when people are in trouble and there is no one to help them, even on occasion political support in oppression,[3] then "fellowship" will look after itself. What matters is to be careful not to confuse means and ends, not to arrange "occasions" for their

· [1] John 15: 15.
[2] Matthew 5: 46.
[3] See Bruce Kenrick, *Come out the Wilderness*.

own sake and then try to find people to partake in them, not to assimilate every sort of need to every other. Above all, it is surely the function of the Church to back people up in their own Christian lives, to let them know that they need not be alone. As Luther put it:[1]

> If anyone be in despair . . . let him go joyfully to the Sacrament˙. . . and seek help from the entire company of the spiritual body and say, "I have on my side Christ's Righteousness, life and sufferings with all the holy angels and all good men upon earth. If I die I am not alone in death. If I suffer, they suffer with me."

A modern catch-phrase is "acceptance" but this can come to seem thin and unfeeling. Tolerance of other people's failings is a great deal, but in the Body of Christ it is rightly felt not to be enough: hence many of our self-conscious efforts after something better. A more useful catch-phrase might be "appreciation", a real attempt to grasp what people are trying to do and be, not just to put up with but to see the point of their peculiarities. If they could feel that the Church was behind them (generally but of course not invariably as exemplified by their parish and its vicar) in their attempts to walk with God and deal with everyday life, then the coffee cups and all they represent would, so to speak, fall into place. The prospect of growing up together "unto a perfect man, unto the measure of the stature of the fulness of Christ" could come to seem much less unrealistic.

[1] Quoted by E. G. Rupp, *The Righteousness of God*, p. 314.

IO

What is Ordination?

VICTOR DE WAAL

I

The position in which the English clergy find themselves today is nicely pinpointed in the two most recent sociological studies on religion in this country, and, interestingly enough, at the place where the authors ostensibly disagree. Dr Bryan Wilson notes "the epiphenomenal character of religious institutions and religious thinking in contemporary society" and argues that such a society is properly called secular, where "by secularization . . . is meant the process whereby religious thinking, practice and institutions lose social significance".[1] Dr David Martin writes, on the contrary, that

> "religion" or "Christianity" is *still* what unites us: the umbrella identification. Just because we are a highly differentiated society in which each group has conflicting interests and psychologies we cannot physically mix in churches (beyond a certain range of social status) and yet require the word "Christian". . . . to symbolise our common membership in the same society. That is why the social action of the churches must be restricted to certain agreed humane objectives which do not raise the crucial dividing issues within or outside religious bodies. Religion provides the obfuscating but necessary rhetoric of public harmony . . . which nobody takes seriously except in relation to the disputes of other people.[2]

Much discussion in recent years has seen the present anxiety of the clergy about their role in society as stemming from the secularizing of most of the functions they used to exercise. The marked increase in the course of the nineteenth-century in their religious quality, their pastoral zeal, and devotion to prayer and to learning, remarked on in Professor Owen Chadwick's first volume on the *Victorian Church*, concealed the beginning of their removal from the centre and leadership of public life.

[1] *Religion in Secular Society*, Watts 1966, pp. xii, xiv.
[2] *A Sociology of English Religion*, SCM Press 1967, pp. 106–07.

They were ceasing to be magistrates; would they not soon cease even to be sought after as counsellors? In the fact of this a "clergy of the gaps" theology of the ministry has not been very consoling, though the inadequacies of the social services are real enough, and it is understandable that many clergy have sought to understand themselves in professional terms. Hence perhaps the eagerness for techniques such as those of "Clinical Theology".

The malaise of the clergy is illuminated from a different angle by Dr Martin's analysis. If religion today is of common necessity excluded from any real involvement in society, then its accredited spokesmen are bound to be restricted, in public expectation, to closely limited roles. And indeed it is common for the clergy to feel their individual humanity threatened by the part in which they know themselves to be cast. People know what they expect from a clergyman in belief and moral precept, and, whatever he may actually be saying, they will reinterpret it in terms of their expectation. If a clergyman is so blunt that reinterpretation is not possible, when, for example, he speaks about politics, the public are outraged. Not so much by the opinion itself as by the fact that it should be proposed by a clergyman. Within the Church itself one aspect of the increasing emphasis on the "ministry of the laity" has been the assumption that a clergyman is not, and should not be, involved in "ordinary life". The psychologically deleterious effect of these attitudes on clergymen's *wives* has almost become a study in itself.

This picture is obviously over-generalized: the pattern of development is not uniform, and there are schools and county towns where the clergy continue to be influential. And it is also exaggerated: all clergymen, if only in private relationships, find means to vary the part imposed on them. But this picture does, I think, help to explain the clergy's continual and sometimes aggressive self-justifying, and their manifest anxiety to be accepted, of which this series of articles on the Ministry in THEOLOGY is itself symptomatic. And it helps to explain the quite extraordinary preoccupation of the clergy with the historical and theological niceties of their own status – witness the discussion about the form of reconciliation between the Anglican and Methodist ministries, and the fear aroused by the modest proposals of the Morley Commission.

That fewer young men of sufficient calibre should wish to engage themselves, and their families, in this career is hardly surprising. They do not see themselves providing "the obfuscating but necessary rhetoric of public harmony". This can safely be left to those who run "the system", the "establishment". Indeed the analogy with politics is striking. If one feels oneself called to work for the improvement of the quality of personal and social living, then the social services and, to a lesser extent, education are the fields chosen, rather than the Church or politics, both of which are thought to be remote from all that is worthwhile in life. That this should be so is certainly disruptive of the traditional concept of Church and State, a circumstance of which the State is at the present time even less aware than the Church.

So it is that our contemporaries, seeking a liberating gospel where they may, look anywhere but to the Church, from which only *stock* responses to the world's questions are expected. Whereas Jesus always seems to have given the *un*expected answer.

II

Every theology of the ministry begins with Jesus. Herein is both its opportunity and its difficulty. Its opportunity, because any doctrine which fails to begin by recognizing the ministry as essentially the ministry of the gospel cannot hope to be adequate; and because the gospel, if it comes to men in their own language and is content that they answer in their own way, is capable of evoking a response in every age. Its difficulty, because the nature of the connexion between Jesus and the functions exercised in the Christian community is liable to misunderstanding.

The perennial Christian instinct has always been to find in Jesus the fulfilment of every ministry, to recognize in him *the* Priest, Prophet, Pastor, Teacher, after whose pattern the Church's ministry is to be exercised. In the same way the piety of those not ordained – many men and all women – has also centred on Jesus, his faith, hope, and love. The *imitatio Christi* has been the moral inspiration of all Christians. On this good foundation, however, has been built a theology of the relation between Jesus and the Church which is more questionable, though it is the one with which we are perhaps most familiar. In this theological model we begin by knowing who exactly Jesus was – the NT records his titles and powers. Some of these, it is then held, he delegated to the apostles and they in their turn to the settled ordained ministry. To the laity he left his inspiration and example, above all of faithful obedience! A theology on these lines is bound to concern itself with ministerial power and status.

Theologians, for example, have held that at the Last Supper Jesus delegated to his apostles his priestly powers of offering the eucharistic sacrifice; at another time he gave them the power of granting or with-holding absolution; at another time the authority to teach, the powers of the *magisterium*; at another time he give specific power to Peter only. As far as delegation in succession to the Apostles is concerned, the disputes between Roman Catholics and Anglicans have in the past centred, not on whether there has in fact been in Hooker's phrase a "lineal descent of power from the Apostles by continued succession of Bishops",[1] but on the exact nature of this power, on whether Anglicans have this succession,

---

[1] *Eccl. Polity*, VII, 14: 11.

and on the question whether or not the Papal power is to be included in the same category. The marked clericalism in certain sections of the constitution on the Church of Vatican II, commented on by Karl Rahner and others, is due to the fact that the much-hailed doctrine of "collegiality" is in fact also based on this long prevalent doctrine, and nourished by the literalist reading of the gospels, on which it is founded.

This model of the connexion between Jesus and the Christian ministry seems to underly also the later developments in the doctrine of sacramental character – the seal, mark, or badge believed to be imprinted on a man's soul by virtue of his baptism, designating him permanently as a Christian before God and the angels. Already in St Augustine we find the idea of character extended to the two other sacraments concerned with a Christian's calling – Confirmation (often by now separated from Baptism in the West) and Ordination. Medieval theologians disputed whether or not this mark persisted into heaven and hell, but they had no doubt about its indelibility on earth, and they distinguished it both from the natural image of God in man, and from the moral likeness of Christ produced in him by sanctifying grace, both of which could be obscured by sin and restored by penance. They agreed that it could not inhere in the very substance of the soul, but argued among themselves which of the rational faculties it marked, some holding with Scotus that it was the will, others with Aquinas that it was the practical reason. As for the question what character actually conferred, the schoolman held that in the subdivision of Aristotle's categories, sacramental character was something akin to the genus of power, a view that confirmed the notion of Christ's delegation of powers. Thus Scotus taught that baptism made us citizens, confirmation soldiers, and ordination officers, an analogy that is still heard today in popular teaching. However, the theological difficulties inherent in trying to distinguish the differences between the character imparted in baptism from that given in confirmation, or in ordination, were always apparent. St Thomas argued for three degrees of priesthood; others held that they corresponded to Christ in his royal, prophetic, and priestly roles respectively. Neither view altogether avoids the difficulty that *full* participation in Christ seems to be reserved to those who have been ordained.

This development may perhaps be traced to the parallel medieval idea of vocation to the religious life, a life devoted to following the evangelical counsels of poverty, chastity, and obedience, which alone could lead to perfection. As this vocation was given to some and not to others, the way was left open for accepting two levels of Christian discipleship. The blurring of the distinction between vocation to the ministry and to the religious life, brought about by the imposition of celibacy on the secular clergy on the one hand and the ordination of all sufficiently literate monks and friars on the other, could therefore well imply that a priest was more fully a Christian than a layman.

III

The unsatisfactory nature of this whole way of explaining the connexion between Jesus and the Christian ministry becomes immediately apparent once we take seriously the light thrown on the NT by critical study. For it seems clear that in his own life-time Jesus refused all titles and designations – even to be called "good" (Mark 10: 18) – and that he instructed his disciples to do likewise (Matt. 23: 8–10). It is doubtful whether he thought of himself as the Suffering Servant or even as the Messiah. Apparently he would only speak of himself, obscurely, as the Son of Man. Again, we cannot now speak in a literal way of his "instituting" the ministry and the sacraments. This, at first sight, very negative conclusion enables us however to make an important theological point: it underlines the originality of Jesus, the newness of the gospel, and helps to safeguard it, as Karl Barth has shown, against any pretension on our part that our religious concepts can completely comprehend him. The Church inherited from Israel, and to a lesser extent from the hellenistic world, religious and social ideas in which alone it could describe its experience of Jesus. But it knew the limitations of its language, it knew that Jesus transcended and revalued the traditional categories. In the NT writings this is expressed by paradox – the secret Messiah, the master washing his slave's feet, the shepherd who is himself the slaughtered lamb, the healer himself in need of healing, above all the king reigning from the gallows – all these turn our values upside down. For our present purpose this means that, while inevitably we can only describe Jesus by extrapolating from our religious concepts, the analogy may not, as it were, be applied in reverse. Jesus did not legitimate these concepts in his turn. Indeed, the author of the Epistle to the Hebrews uses the metaphor of an Eternal Priest offering the sacrifice once for all of his own blood, more effective than that of sacrificial animals, in order to argue that priesthood and sacrifice in the old sense are outmoded by the advent of Christ.

We have therefore to seek another model to help us understand the connexion between Jesus and the Christian ministry. And I suggest that we can do no better than begin with St Paul's doctrine of the body of Christ in 1 Corinthians 12 and Ephesians 4, which he adapted from the stoic idea of the body of mankind. It is a meagre anthropology which fails to approach the understanding of man in the context of the community of which he is a part and in which only he can live and grow. Similarly any theology which treats christology, the vocation of the individual Christian, and the doctrine of the Church, in separation is bound to distort all three. Our present confusion and difficulties about the ministry are a direct consequence of this distortion, for we seem often to be trying to relate Jesus and the ministry out of the context of the Christian community. The fact is of course that much of our church life notoriously lacks just such a communal context. The communal nature of the Church, in the straightforward sense of a group whose members meet and know one another, is nowhere clearer than in the use from the NT onwards, and often remarked on, of the words *Corpus Christi* to designate both the eucharistic gift and the Christian community. This indicates that the Church is most readily understood for what it is when it is assembled for the eucharist. Already in the OT the "assembly", meeting together in one place, is thought of as fundamental to Israel, as is witnessed by the desire to gather in Jerusalem for the great festivals, a principle extended and necessarily mitigated by regarding the synagogue as a reflection of the Temple. Again, both Jewish and Christian eschatology has always thought of the end in terms of a general assize. Thus, while the word *qahal*, variously translated as *ekklesia*, assembly, or church, came in fact to designate God's people only theoretically assembled, as it were in his sight, the basic idea of actual meeting was never totally abandoned. And it is this aspect that takes on new life and meaning in the Church, to which, as to the idealized nomadic Israel of old, God has promised his presence night and day. It is in this light that we must read the NT writers' interpretation of Jesus' body as the new Temple, and their accounts of the Last Supper, the promise of the Paraclete, and the Resurrection appearances, which are nearly all in the context of eucharistic meals. As Dom Gregory Dix pointed out so forcefully, the early Christians, even in the virtual certainty of arrest, clung to the eucharistic *assembly* (not just to Holy Communion which they could have had privately) as to a life line, for without it they did not constitute the Church of Jesus Christ.[1] We can see in retrospect how, as the eucharist came less and less to be the sharing together of the common loaf, the model of the Church as Christ's body becomes a mere theological fiction. The sense of Christ's presence becomes localized, to be worshipped from afar, the preserve of the clergy who alone communicate regularly.

The critical point was reached, as Fr J. P. Audet, OP has argued,[2] when the "communauté de base", the fundamental Christian group, ceased to be the familial household and became the public basilica. The effect of this on the form and functions of the ministry was profound. Family instruction becomes public rhetoric, the family meal becomes "refreshments" served by professional caterers. Whereas before all the participants know one another intimately and the father has direct contact with all, now we have a formal speech and personal greetings inevitably only for a few: for the number of people involved necessarily affects both the form and the content of human relationships. While St Paul develops the ecumenical and eschatalogical perspective of the vocation of God's people, already hinted at in the OT, the basic group that he takes for granted is still the

---

[1] *The Shape of the Liturgy*, Dacre Press 1945, pp. 151–52.
[2] *Mariage et Célibat dans le service pastoral de l'Eglise*, Paris, 1967. Summarized in *Maintenant*, November 1967.

familial house church, in which men and women can grow by mutual edification into the moral stature of Christ. He recognizes that just as in any group there will be a variety of talents, so in the Christian community there will be different functions. But for him necessary order becomes sacred order, and he teaches that different aptitudes are to be interpreted as spiritual gifts, i.e. gifts of the risen Christ, and that they should be respected as such, for each man and woman has his particular vocation from God (1 Cor. 12: 14–30).

The Christian community, like any group, is bound to make use of the talents within it in order to fulfil its own inner needs and to respond to the outside pressures to which it is subjected. Some of these needs and pressures are perennial, some will change. At first leadership may pass readily between various members, depending on the demands of the moment; later, as structures inevitably harden, there will be permanent officials, but even so the functions they exercise may alter with the times.

Thus have Bishop and Presbyter often shared or even exchanged functions, thus has the Presbyter in the West swallowed up the Deacon. So too has the official ministry absorbed the charismatic and, in the days of clericalism, also the ministry of the layman. But leadership of whatever sort can never exist in its own right. Because its genesis and purpose is to enable the group to fulfil itself, it is bound to reflect the concerns and characteristics of that group. The Church's leaders have had neutral titles – overseer, elder, servant (chairman, committee member, secretary, as we would say today). They have taken on their colour, their richness of significance, from the Christian body which itself in its wholeness is vivified by the new life of the gospel, by the transforming life of the Spirit. The word "hierarchy", long employed of priestly and episcopal rule over the Church, needs to be restored to its older patristic usage and meaning – the sacred order of all God's people.

It follows that before we can speak meaningfully, for example, of ministerial authority in the Church we have to recognize that the Church is neither an autocracy nor a democracy, but makes its abiding decisions synodically, that is by reaching a common mind; and that in this process the whole Christian tradition plays its part, in its manifold strands – scripture, creeds, liturgy, ethics. Similar considerations apply when we turn to the *magisterium*, the Church's teaching office. The traditional distinction between the *ecclesia docens* and the *ecclesia discens* is an arbitrary one, for there are many life situations when any ordinary Christian assumes the role of the former. Again the mutual care that Christians should have for one another and for the outcast is primary to any pastoral office. Likewise, only within or on the basis of a Church that is dedicated to the truth, to intellectual integrity, to setting men morally free, can there be genuine prophecy; and only as part of a community concerned with reconciliation and forgiveness in the unity of truth and justice, of offering itself and its world in eucharist through Christ to the Father, can there be a ministry that is truly priestly.

Conversely, the psychological impoverishment of the clergy, which I sketched at the outset, is in large measure due to the anaemic state of the Church's corporate life. If to call the Church "God's household, the pillar and bulwark of the truth" (1 Tim. 3: 15) sounds curiously inappropriate, if to designate it "a chosen race, a royal priesthood, a dedicated nation, God's people proclaiming his triumphs" (1 Pet. 2: 9) seems a pathetic boast, and if it is sheer fantasy to call Christians "kings and priests" (Rev. 1: 6), then the pretensions and trappings of its leaders will naturally take on an air of unreality and make-believe, and their authority will appear hollow. And there is little consolation in the fact that the English are lovers of make-believe, and experts at it (witness the superb royal, civic and capitular ceremonies in our cathedrals, which surpass any presented by the Royal Shakespeare Theatre).

IV

When, therefore, we come to ask what is meant by "ordination", we are concerned, in the specific context of the Christian community, with the interrelationship between a group and the leadership of that group. The nature of that interrelationship may be summarized as follows. On the one hand the group, in order to continue its life and develop its concerns, calls for certain sorts of leadership; on the other, different members of the group contribute their own particular aptitudes. In choosing and appointing its leaders, therefore, whether formally or informally, the group authorizes them to employ these talents to further its purposes, and clothes them, as it were, with its own characteristics. Thus ordination presupposes both a vocation, "directly" from God, in the sense that he endows an individual with certain gifts, and mediately "through the Church" in its selection of him to exercise certain of its functions. It is worth noting here that the Church, except at its worst moments, has never acted as if the grace of holy orders were a substitute for natural aptitudes, but, as is testified already in the Pastoral Epistles, has always sought for specific qualities in those it puts forward for ordination. The ordination itself is first a prayer that God will endorse this choice by enabling the ordinand to fulfil and persevere in the functions allotted to him, and secondarily, and by implication, the public authorization and commission of the man concerned. Ordination is a public testimony that the ministry he is to exercise in and for the Church is to be none other than that of the unchanging gospel. "Jesus Christ, the same yesterday and today and for ever" (Heb. 13: 8). As Bishop Westcott said in his commentary on John 20: 21,

> The Lord presents His own Mission as the one abiding Mission of the Father; this He fulfils through His church. His disciples receive no new commission, but

carry out His. . . . They are not (in this respect) His envoys, but in a secondary degree envoys of the Father.[1]

It is this belief, and not any doctrine of delegation, which we can discern in the NT when we find Jesus designated "Apostle and High Priest" (Heb. 3:1) or "Shepherd and Bishop" (1 Peter 2:25); and again in early ordination prayers when a bishop is ordained with a prayer for the out-pouring of the "princely" and "high-priestly Spirit" which his Father bestowed on Jesus, or a deacon with a prayer that he may "minister" as Christ "ministered".[2] And this, too, is the concern of Irenaeus and others when against the Gnostics he speaks of succession from the apostles, a concern which finds parallel expression in the formulation of the NT Canon and the first Creeds.

For all the strangeness for us today of its philosophical presuppositions, we can perhaps now see the intention of the doctrine of sacramental character. The uniqueness of baptism reflects for the individual Christian the uniqueness of Christ and his work. The Christian's life has been transformed by the gospel, it echoes the newness of Jesus. The NT analogies are familiar: the Christian is said to participate figuratively in the death, burial, and resurrection of the Lord; he is born again, converted, forgiven, liberated; he is imbued with the Spirit, he puts on Christ. Henceforward he lives in the new age, in the time of the end, he is a citizen of heaven. Here is no room for the old order of ceaseless repetition, of "year by year". What Christ has done for each one he has done once for all.

When the doctrine of indelible character is extended to ordination, nothing less is implied, it seems to me, but also nothing more, than that a man's ministry is inseparable from his calling as a Christian, and that for a particular time and place a man's vocation is bound to assume a specific form. For him to exercise a particular function will be his faithful Christian response, and from this response there is no turning back. Hence the instinctive refusal of the Church to ordain a second time any more than it would rebaptize. This view of the ministry also exposes the clericalist assumptions underlying much recent writing on the so-called "ministry", "priesthood", or "apostolate" of the laity. For all the excellence of its emphasis on individual Christian responsibility, such a theology, by conceiving of the laity, not as the whole people of God, but merely as those who are not ordained, makes a coherent account of leadership in the Christian community impossible and has largely con-tributed to the lack of "vocations" to the ministry, for the young have little inclination to lead from behind. The fact that the clergy are restricted and isolated, however respectfully, to their studies, to the exercise of their "sacramental powers", and to encouraging the faithful, while these

[1] *The Gospel according to St John*, p. 359.
[2] Hippolytus, *Apostolic Tradition*, ad loc.

latter are thought of as fulfilling an authentic ministry in the "real" world, is, by a stroke of historical irony, no doubt largely due to the ministry developing its own professional ethos. And this in turn is the accidental result of a paid or "full-time" ministry, which for whole periods of the history of some churches has been a convenient arrangement when the ecclesiastical organization has been large. It is far from my purpose to suggest that we should despise this professional ethos, for it has produced some of the finest examples of Christian discipleship. Moreover, the "full-time" ministry continues to provide society at large with a few men who, being uncommitted to its structures, can exercise a healthy critique of its "ladders" and can mediate within it. When this is possible, this remains the most attractive aspect of the "amateur" character of the clergy. But we have to recognize its negative concomitant, namely that many of the clergy live and work in situations where they only meet Christians. If the non-Christian world, which is a daily reality to the unordained, is for most of their leaders on or over the distant horizon, the psychological effects on priorities and policy are obvious. And for many who are in positions of isolation, the old clerical piety, which accepted loneliness as part of the priestly vocation, no longer consoles. For theirs is not the loneliness of the pioneer apostle, but the isolation of those who sense that they are being squeezed out of society, which, in according them the title of "reverend", includes them in the same category as other antique and picturesque functionaries left over from a former age.

V

If then, in conclusion, I may speak hesitatingly about the future, it would seem that the ordained ministry is likely to rediscover its nature and functions, only in so far as the Church comes to terms with itself again as a voluntary association, and is prepared to live more of its life at the level of groups where its members can really meet, know, and help one another, and so together serve Christ in the world. The signs that this has in fact already been happening for some time are not far to seek. And here some words of the Jesuit theologian Karl Rahner (speaking to students at Freiburg University in 1965 about the Church of the future) are appropriate.

> We are all one in Christ, the ultimate difference is the degree of love, for God and the brothers; distinctions of office are necessary but entirely secondary and provisional, a burden, a service, a sacred responsibility. . . . The bishop will not look very different from any other official in a small voluntary group effectively dependent on the good will of that group. . . . It will be clear and plain to see, that all dignity and office in the Church is uncovenanted service, carrying with it no honour in the world's eyes . . . perhaps it will no longer constitute a profession in the social and secular sense at all.[1]

[1] Quoted in *Herder Correspondence*, July 1965.

I I

The Ministry to Immigrant Communities

THE BISHOP OF MASHONALAND

We speak of the Church and the immigrant, we discuss new aspects of the pastoral ministry in relation to newcomers to our shores. But, in doing so, we too easily forget that this is an almost incredibly ancient story and one which prophet, priest and king have always had to contend with.

For nothing has been recorded that is older than migration. Men were nomads and dwelt in caves and tents when history first discovered them, and, before this, before the Ice-man came, there was always a life and death compulsion to seek a place near the sun – or away from its too fierce heat.

Almost from the first, moreover, the migrant was a manly, respectable figure. Abel, the nomad seeking new pastures for his flocks, was respectable even in the sight of the Lord – so claims the writer of Genesis, and, in the same breath, denounces Cain who stayed at home and tilled the ground. Nor can anyone doubt that the young Esau, also a wandering migrant, was a more attractive character than Jacob, the city-slicker, who stayed at home and traded in pottage.

But values have changed. Though the migrant Rechabites were noble because they were under a vow not to build houses and inhabit them, but endlessly to travel on, in most ages since then civilization itself has been thought noble, and to be civilized a man had to stay in his *civis*, his city-state. The alternative was to be a Pagan. Thus the civilized man has fled the land as starlings do at dusk, sweeping into the warmth and chatter of great cities. Empire builders and adventurers have often carried the benefits of civilization out again to far off places, but they, the immigrants such as Cecil Rhodes or the traders of the East India Company, were always able to silence anti-immigrant demonstrations by being richer than the demonstrators, and so spinning wide around them a web of economic prosperity. Nothing· succeeds like success, and British immigrants in far away lands were always successful, often beyond their own dreams, for nearly four hundred years. They were successful because they were brave, because they were resourceful to a masterly degree, and because they were very frequently honourable, sometimes humane, occasionally self-sacrificing. Imperial immigrants were by no means always devils.

But, among immigrants, whether because the Ice-man came or the city beckoned, whether at an Imperial Durbar or among the shacks of Algerians around Paris today, the family has always been the factor of greatest significance. The priest or social worker who has concern for immigrants in our day in this country needs constantly to remember that it is the family here, or still back home, which forms the real world in the mind of the immigrant. In Britain he probably lives in a faceless part of the down-town city where community life has no meaning. His family may not carry the sanctity of the marriage bond, but the bonds that knit him to meaning in life are the bonds of family.

Very frequently among the migrants of history the family has been most significant by its absence, an absence putting intolerable strain and stress upon marital and filial love and duty. But, as an incentive to a tremendous effort to succeed, it is the family, present or absent, which has caused men to exploit the natives, whether they be natives of Rhodesia or Birmingham, whether in old days by the crack of a whip or in modern days by fiddling the Inland Revenue concerning the number of one's children back in Karachi. And, for the family, men have not only exploited the natives, but fought with them for a house or a job, or, out of love for wife and children left them behind and for ten years endured the natives alone. From love for the family that was not there, immigrants have died in an attic in Notting Hill or a desert in Africa. Uncertain of everything else except that the family mattered, immigrants, who have left behind them many countries including Britain, have endured and will endure more than the natives will suffer. For want of their families I have seen Englishmen die in a prison camp in Japan and West Indians die amid plenty in Birmingham.

"You see, Reverend," said a young Barbadian, "If you's young and .got a wife and kids, and you know that the cane crop don't want you for more than six months in the year and that after that you had was to live on what you saved, if you've got any guts and can see an opening up in England, you take it."

It is not only when the sugar prices fall in Barbados, or the five thousand bicycle rickshaws in Jullundur city in the Punjab fail, with their dismal profits, to support the family, that men move. If politics is the art of the possible, more so is migration, and in Britain since the second world war immigrants have arrived because of blue airletter forms travelling home to tell someone in the family that it is possible. Most immigrants have been "sent for" by someone in the family. This is why the very great majority of Indian or Pakistani immigrants to Britain have come from one or two areas which are tiny in relation to the size of the sub-continent. Ask almost any Indian in the Midlands how far his village is from Jullundur city, and the answer will seldom be more than twenty miles. Of course the very poor, who are the great majority, can never migrate from India or Pakistan or Africa, for there the term poverty means a way of life which almost all Europe has forgotten. For them to emigrate is not, even in their dreams, the art of the possible.

Thus, although immigration is a fierce issue both of genuine politics and also of band-waggoneering; though it is a force in the economy of most countries at ground level; yet, in terms of ultimate values it is as a principal factor of family life that it is of the first importance. If immigration is used to ensure a fluid labour force or to gain the floating vote it will produce the kind of instability that those watery terms deserve. It is a family matter, that of the family far away and the family down our street, the family at home and the family next door with whom somebody's children grow up. It is basically in these terms that the ministry of the Church, ordained and lay, must be active in a multi-racial community. It is towards the family also that the committee of the local Sikh Gurdwara and the local Muslim Association will be directing its concern. How vital it is that there should be a *rapport* between all three (and perhaps the Vedic Centre) if the Christian Church is to address itself to the specifically social aspect of a ministry to migrants.

In a city like Birmingham a far higher percentage of migrants than English people will worship God on a Sunday. If one includes the Irish Roman Catholics and the worshippers at the Gurdwara in Smethwick and the Muslims at the end of Ramadan and the sundry Poles, Yugoslavs and Greek Cypriots, it is probably true that without percentage and on a directly numerical basis the English who go to a place of worship are in a minority. For all these people religion is so closely tied to culture, country and family that an intellectual approach or anything which could be called theology in modern language will not easily be heard. For a West Indian there may be a moment of intense reality even in a very infrequent Communion, and a nostalgic sense of "going home" in the words of a psalm, a hymn, a Prayer Book collect or a phrase of the Bible (AV only). He wants either deep emotion or impeccable respectability in religion and this is far more important to him than mere intellectual honesty. The poorer people of Barbados sometimes stand around the open windows of their cathedral if they are not well enough dressed to enter the doors. But they will insist that the alms-bag be passed to them as they cluster outside. And God is not mocked.

In the immigrant parish, then, concern for the family must be paramount and an acceptance of worship in Church and prayer in the home can be demanded even though it appears "merely" emotion or "merely" respectable. Vast numbers of immigrants will lapse from the practices of their faith, but only a tiny minority will cease to believe that worship and prayer are the proper norm when life is normal. "But it hasn't been normal since we left home."

It is all too easy to worry over immigration into Britain for the wrong reasons. There *is* a housing problem. But immigrants have built more houses than they live in, and the problem is largely that of modern industry scrambling for congested space and so demanding that too many workers live in too few and too narrow areas of city growth.

There are grave education problems, but they stem from the early polyglot stage of migration, from the way in which all cities tend to force all "problem" families, English or foreign, to live "down-town". Immigrant parents need urgently to be encouraged to provide books and paper for their children to read at home, and the lack of them often holds back education. But, apart from this, and once language differences have been overcome, it is difficult to understand why there is more of an educational problem if a school is "nearly all coloured", than if it is "nearly all white".

Again, there are deep and intractable problems of subtle as well as open discrimination in such matters as jobs, insurance and accommodation for a coloured family in almost any holiday resort. Laity are better placed than their clergy in standing against these things. Legislation can never cure them by itself and in some instances may inflame the situation. The pace of advance is, finally, the pace at which we translate the Lord's Prayer from our lips to our lives. This is not just a problem of immigration but a problem of what, in simpler days, could be called the problem of original sin.

During this past summer a building contractor in a great cathedral city sent word through the Church to Birmingham that it was time that they had a few immigrants in his part of the world and that he would interview and employ a few if they travelled across at his expense to see him. This startlingly unusual process has begun. At much the same time a country rector in Herefordshire wrote and offered a week's holiday for an immigrant family. The effect of this being taken up was a new attitude on life for the immigrant family and a not inconsiderable one on the village concerned. This is the realistic level of race relations, though few will rise to it, and a degree in social sciences cannot bring it about.

Immigration has meant and will always mean deep problems of social misunderstanding, of wide incompatibility in a neighbourhood, and that jealousy and greed which look so much worse in peoples whose motives and thoughts and culture one cannot clearly interpret. Here the Church has a patient and prophetic role to play. It can help by informing public opinion. How many people realize that today the Health Service (41 per cent of hospital doctors come from overseas) could not continue without immigrants and the second-generation coloured English? Transport services, the foundries of the motor industry and the wool trade of Bradford are also today dependent upon them absolutely.

All these problems, for the immigrant as for the "host" community, stem from fear because the family may be hurt or denied its rights. It requires the whole Gospel ever to still fears. The family may be threatened equally because it has always lived in this particular area and now "they" have come, or because it is newly-arrived and is vulnerable to all the vested interests that surround it. There is, too, that other fear which wells out of loneliness into a blazing hatred against society and to a desire to assert oneself at someone's expense. There is the rage of loneliness because our neighbourhood is changing, the city planners have bull-dozed away our landmarks and community life has vanished even from the pub. There is the rage of loneliness because the family is not there but is struggling back in Biafra or Asia or the Caribbean while the rain falls on Birmingham.

Here are three letters from men from overseas who have had this rage of loneliness running through them and which caused in these three instances crime, sickness and, in the third, a stubborn, couragous, church-going.

"Des", from Montserrat, once a server in his church, wrote from a Borstal in Suffolk:

> I received your letter and was more than glad to hear from you. I had a letter from my Mam last week and she says that my father isn't coming over here any more, because there is a new doctor from here is over there now. And he went to see him about his stomach and the doctor said to him that if he wants to get better it would cost him £400 nicker, and where he is going to get that much I dont no, becuase I am not out to help them so I reckon they are having a hard time without me because I am the only one that could do anything And I am in here. . . .

The second letter was from a man who has, by his sister's generosity, now succeeded in returning to Barbados which was, perhaps, all that he really required but which so few migrants dare acknowledge because "you can't go as you came".

> Dear Revnd, Sir I am asking you kindly to come and give me a word of Pray, I am still Real ill with my stomach, I was taken to the queen Elizabeth Hospital on Monday last I was very bad, they taken Ex-Ray of my stomach and chest but I have to wait until Tuesday to see what is the result of it, Please would you come and give me a word of Pray soon Please I ask, Sir, God will bless you. I am suffering with my stomach very bad, till I cant work to send any money for my wife and 5 kids, I real suffering myself and them as well, Please come to my help Revnd, I am looking for you next week, Please God,
>
> From M. D. Russell
> God bless us

it seems to me like a very serious case, I told the doctor, he says when the x-ray

come, then he will do to suit. I dont feel able to work again in England, not how
my stomach feel.

In fact, when the doctor saw the X-ray there was nothing at all that
he had to "do to suit", for even modern X-ray apparatus does not show
up a man's anxieties about his wife and five kids, nor has a hospital a cure
for it.

The third of these three letters was from Charles, whose devoted wife
and many children I had met in St Kitts. Now two of the boys have
joined him and life is much better. But until then, in spite of his enormous,
gusty laughter which pleased everyone, Charles was quite lost without
any of his family, and a poor hand at looking after himself. So unable
to make a home was he, that he moved from shabby room to shabby
room fourteen times in four years. Once, admittedly, a fire which might
have killed him and did injure him drove him out of a tiny attic. He
wrote to report this, ". . . all I come away with is two shoes, both for
de left foot (laugh), but God is good. . . ."

After his eleventh move he wrote:

> Good day, How are you keeping, I hope good. I guest your fairly busy preparing
> for Christmas. Blessed is the man that endureth temptation for when he is tried
> he shall receive the crown of life. This is news for you I am sorry to say Mr Johnson
> have given me my discharge to leave his house. He said he dont like me to sing in
> the house. I do love singing wherever I goes. But I dont believe it is because I sing
> on him, but its the kind of life I see he is living, a racketaring life through having
> a car. Knowing the work he does in the church I speak to him about it. After
> speaking to him he is ashame, he comes in the house and meets me and dont
> speak to me. I will sing while he is vex and he discharge me. Nevertheless I will
> locate a some where and will let you know later, I will have courage for the Lord
> knoweth how to deliver the godly out of temtation wishing you all lots and lots
> and lots of love and a joyous Christmas.

At the heart of those three letters is a cry of loneliness in parting from
the family, and it is a reminder that, in Britain, the parish church with
immigrants nearby has a first responsibility to provide fellowship and
individual care. It is far from easy; it needs to be done in conjunction
with secular social services, the local authority and any gatherings of
people of other than Christian faith. It can all too easily pass into mere
welfare work. But, as yet, all immigrants have a culture which allows a
place for the worship of God – an emotional and respectable aspect of life
not in tune with the modern, sophisticated West. But some fulfilment in
worship and the satisfaction of meaningful family life are the two things
without which no politics, social welfare nor programme of emancipa-
tion can take the sting out of race relations in the cosmopolitan societies
of the twentieth century.

12

The Town Parson

ALAN ECCLESTONE

Sir, the life of a parson, of a conscientious clergyman, is not easy. I have always considered a clergyman as the father of a larger family than he is able to maintain. I would rather have Chancery suits upon my hands than the cure of souls.

SAMUEL JOHNSON, 1778

The difficulties of the fathers of these inordinately swollen families have grown rather than diminished in the years since Dr Johnson made his comment. They have grown, not only because the conditions in which the parson is set to work have become more complex and more difficult to handle, but also because the perception or definition of the job to be done has been incompetently dealt with by the Church. It is a truism of this age that, in business and administration, efficiency depends to a very great extent upon the correct definition of the jobs which men are expected to do. Pioneers admittedly must create new jobs, but the pioneering itself begins from perception of new problems. In the life of the Church, as it entered the age of increasing urbanization, both delineation of new problems and definition of new jobs were largely neglected. The town parson is a man now saddled with the consequences of such neglect. Asa Briggs has brilliantly described the ambivalent attitudes of men faced in the past century and a half by the cities they had created. Pride and fear, irresolution and determination, seem almost equally balanced, so that a stop-go procedure marks the history of civic initiative.[1] That the Church authorities were more afraid of the towns and cities than secular reformers were helped to make matters worse. Today's town parson is, in Sydney Smith's words, "a man thrown into life with his hands tied, and bid to swim; he does well if he keeps his head above water".

In the background of Anglican piety there stands the attractive figure of George Herbert's country parson whose life and work, a pastoral

[1] Asa Briggs, *Victorian Cities*, 1963.

95

idyll, were, notwithstanding the upheavals of the Reformation, the out-come of a long maturing process. Behind the Herbert portrait stretch generations of men who ministered to small communities whose life and rhythms were slow-moving and familiar. The parson could know each member of his flock, as Richard Gough shows in his history of the parish of Myddle, with delightful intimacy. The Church of England has no comparable picture of the town parson. It cannot have one because the community and the time-span needed to shape such a person have not been forthcoming. All too often Little Gidding and Bemerton have held the imagination, and a good deal of the confusion which surrounds the parson's job today derives from the romantic glow, sustained by piety and nostalgia, which attaches itself to pre-urbanized modes of living.

The Church was not singular in this failure to grasp the nature of the social revolution which nineteenth-century urbanization brought about. We could notice and ponder the belated efforts made in the creation of county and borough councils, urban and rural districts, and even parish councils, by the civil authority, to give some kind of socio-political structure, some foundation for community life, to the masses of people herded together by the industrialization of the country. We could compare such efforts with the belated subdivision and mutiplication of town parishes and the tardy creation of new dioceses undertaken by the Church.

So, the town parson was set to do an impossible job. Lacking the help of a corporate body sensitive to the new conditions, it fell to individual men to make what sense they could of the job. Like so many Robinson Crusoes they built the town parish-church life as best they could. The heroic work of slum priests, the campaigns of fervent preachers, the adaptation to town life of the old patterns of clerical behaviour went on, a mission zeal was generated, and an outpouring of energy together with the building of great numbers of new churches contrived to hide the truth of the situation. It was the assumptions of all this energetic work which needed examination. Charles Booth's picture of the patchwork quilt effect of it in the parishes of London given in his famous Survey provides its own sad commentary on something often magnificent – but not war. It was so comparable with the Charge of the Light Brigade. What was lacking was widespread concerted wrestling with objectives, methods, initiatives, proper to these town conditions. F. D. Maurice who was alive enough to feel the painful impact of this rapidly changing society upon the Christian Church was none the less rigidly opposed to thinking in dynamic terms about the situation. "Society is not to be made new by arrangement of ours," he wrote, "but is to be regenerated by finding the law and crown of its order and harmony, the only secret of its existence, in God." To discover that secret he looked back not forward. The town parson, so far from being helped to grapple with his new conditions, was actually hindered by the continued acceptance by the majority of people of the image of the parson derived from the past. The picture of a "good parson" described by Dickens in the figure of the Reverend Frank Milvey in *Our Mutual Friend* would still have been the popular image down to 1914 or after.

We stand now on the edge of a new situation. If we will, we can have our eyes opened, and thus be compelled to make radical decisions about the ministry in the towns. Social studies have now done much to redress the balance in terms of knowledge of the town and the life of town dwellers, to define the problems, to assess the resources. They make clear that we have to run a good deal faster in order to keep up with the demands of the changing conditions. Harvey Cox and others have begun to provide the necessary theological critiques of the situation. "We have affirmed technopolitan man in his pragmatism and in his profanity." Herbert Richardson, in his *Theology for a New World*, has affirmed still more: namely, that since America has created the new kind of social knowledge appropriate to the age of sociotechnics, American theology is shaping the necessary "intellectus" which is demanded by this age. God is no less responsible for, no less concerned about, no less to be found in, the town than, as heretofore, in the country. We can learn to see, if we will, that the agenda is set by the streets, factories, entertainments and traffic rather than by the ecclesiastical institutions and theological presuppositions of the past. We can learn from the French worker-priests that it is not only the agenda but also the course of action to be followed that is shaped by the engagement with the working life of the city. "The Christian does not select his method. His mode of action is imposed upon him by the environment into which he is plunged", provided that this Christian is willing to be detached enough from the traditional actions which have hitherto occupied his attention. We can, if we will, develop a self-criticism which can lay bare both the overhang of the past and the otherwise concealed changes going on in the life of the town church, both of which confuse purpose, sap energies and divert attention from the critical issues.

Do we will it? Do we see the situation in these radical terms? There is little evidence at national level of a willingness to overhaul the whole approach to the problem of the town parishes. The best we have in this direction consists of experimental ministries in industry and specialized fields. We have had at least one much publicized high-powered engagement with the town life written up and written off as a failure. At the local level, it is most probable that the town congregations to which clergymen still go don't will anything of the kind. The parson they want is the man who will make a "success" of the church life they already know. They want the fashionable aggregate of organizations grouped round the parish church and giving it an appearance of vitality to be maintained; a favourable balance of payments, a parson to fill the pews. A great number of men are, with varying degress of depression and sickness of

heart, trying to meet these demands. A growing company of younger
men are wondering how much longer they can go on in such a ministry.
A sizeable number of them are already pulling out of it. The more
sensitive men in all these groups know that the shape, direction, outlook,
and methods of town-parish work conceived of in such terms verge on
futility. They know that outside and beyond these narrowly parochial
enclaves the structures and agencies of modern society perform their
functions neither aided by nor challenged by the town parson and his
people, paying less attention to them than Julius Caesar did to sooth-
sayers and augurs. Nothing short of a radical reassessment of the town
parson's job is going to make any difference to this slide towards nullity.
Such reassessment will promise no spectacular gains, hold out no exaggerated hopes, but rather compel a greater honesty of vision.

How to begin? There is some ground to be cleared first of all. The
counsel and observation of Moses' father-in-law is relevant here. The
town parson has to be freed from the burden of trying to be too many
men in one, and this calls for a rethinking of the whole pattern of the
ministry of the Church. Such rethinking was touched upon by Coleridge
in his reflections upon a new clerisy long ago, but little was done to work
out the implications of it. We still speak and think of priesthood as the
type and image of ministry and then subsequently find men asking
themselves whether they were ordained priests to do the jobs they find
themselves doing. When laymen are moved to consider their own
ministry in the Church they tend to be over-impressed by the character
of priesthood with which they have become familiar, and so they
gravitate all too easily towards the clerical pattern.

Have we not to start thinking in terms of "orders" quite other and
different from the traditional bishop–priest–deacon ministry? These are
inadequate. In the two centuries of intensive urbanization which have
spotlighted the problem of the town parson not one of these orders has
retained an immediacy of engagement with the work to be done. The
diaconate has been largely gutted of meaning; the episcopate stretched to
fantastically unreal lengths; the priesthood saddled with as many expectations as the White Knight in the Looking-Glass land. "New occasions teach new duties" and presumably call for new ministries. Simply
to overload the already existing ones is to destroy their efficacy. We come
back to the problem of definition. The apostles rightly protested against
being deflected from their proper work, and the Church of that age
appears to have taken steps to meet the problem. We have not taken the
lesson. The new orders that are called for must not be thought of as
subordinate to the traditional ones but as of equal importance and dignity,
and the terms employed in the act of ordination must be as weighty and
expressive as those which the Ordinal uses for the ancient offices within
the Church. If we have not seriously begun to think of such orders –
and the kind of atmosphere in which the ministry of women is discussed

suggests that we haven't – should we not ask ourselves whether this does not indicate a failure in imagination, a failure to grasp the immensity of the work of the Church in the modern world.

Looking at the situation of the town parson today, we should be aware of two great features which bear heavily upon his work and call for new attempts to meet the problems connected with town life. The parish was once a unit of corporate life. It is hardly such today in towns. The agencies which organize, control and direct the industrial, educational, social and cultural life of the people are centred in national, regional or corporative points remote from the parish horizons. The decisions which affect the lives of the people inside a parish are made in half-a-dozen places elsewhere. The parish as such is rarely in a position to make any comment upon the process of decision-making. The internal structure of the parish has altered, too. Within it there are likely to be a dozen or more points at which local interests are shaped without the slightest reference to the parish church, its people and its priest. Brian Jackson's study of Huddersfield entitled *Working Class Community* (1968) makes very clear the presence of what he calls a "mesh of groups" midway between the home and family units on the one hand and the trade unions, chapels, churches, co-ops, etc., on the other. These groups include the brass bands, the social clubs, the bowling greens, the jazz clubs, all brought into being by their members for the satisfaction of local interests and needs. They create the cultural environment immediately influential upon their members. They occupy the leisure, time and energy of great numbers of people. They co-exist more or less peacefully because they can ignore each other. It is into this category of interest that the town church tends to be pushed. It comes to be thought of as catering, like the brass band, for those who like "that sort of thing". It may well become as self-centred as the bowling club. To make matters worse, within the church group a mesh of even smaller units devoted to still narrower concerns may grow up. The larger the aggregates of population, the more the process of part-time segregation gathers strength, and the principle of anonymity described by Harvey Cox in *The Secular City* operates to make more and more people unaware of, indifferent to, the cultural centres of other people's lives. This may be inescapable so far, but where does the town parson stand in relation to this process? Far from being in person a focal point of common life among the people, he becomes a peripheral figure to great numbers whose community interests he cannot share. His functions in the Occasional Offices, potentially of deep significance, are too intermittent if unsupported by other contacts, to counteract this trend which sets the parson apart from the popularly conceived and popularly run groups, and his well-meant efforts to overcome this may even be regarded as attempts to win support for "his" church and part of a struggle to survive.

This is a depressing condition for any man who would be "all things to all men" if only he could see the way to do it. It is understandable that many a town-parson becomes engrossed in the congregation and its survival in the face of the general genial indifference with which the majority of townspeople greet him. He is made very conscious that "the Church has been driven into the purely private sector of this society where she seemed at least to be assured of an independent existence"[1]. What is called for here is straightforward acceptance of the fact that a great many of the old assumptions of the paron's calling have to be stripped off as a necessary stage in the formulation of a workable ministry. He will be freed from dead things. Any kind of paternalism, any authoritarian attitudes, any arrogance, has to go; and we do well to remember that arrogance is the note that English novelists associate with clergymen. But having said that, the job is there with an overwhelming importance.

This town parson, freed from trying to be what other ministries must undertake, will then be able to be that compound prophet-priest that is now needed so desperately in towns. He will be free to work out the new kind of ministry that it calls for. Two stages may be distinguished. The first concerns the area of activity set up by the local church. Here his job is that of guidance from within. He must in very truth become so much within it that he is absorbed into it, and yet and because of this, able to stimulate it towards the job to be done by the Church as a whole. Can it become a body sensitive to the nature and problems of the town life in which it is immersed? Can it become the body intelligent enough to make true comment upon what is going on there? Can it become service-able to this town life at points that cry out for help? It will only do so if the parson himself is prepared to try to shape his ministry so that it becomes part of a corporate ministry, not simply of other clergymen, but of the whole body of the local church. His must be a part that helps to make conscious, articulate, purposeful, the experience of all the other members. The emphasis here is on "helps" because anything that savours of imposing on that experience what the clergyman might want it to look like, or what he imagines it to be like, will be fatal to genuine encounter with contemporary society. The trouble is that clericalism is so influential. The town parson now has to empty himself in order to encourage his church members to be both sensitive to and honest about the real conditions of modern life, helping them to acquire, through regular and frequent review of the experience of the church people, some standards, insights, perspectives, of human life which will equip them to be discerning and discriminating as they go about their daily working life. He has to help all the Lord's people to be receptive enough to be prophets if and when needed. Opening the eyes of the blind was one of the declared and practised purposes of Jesus Christ. Town life

[1] Adolfs, *The Grave of God.*

has for generations bred its own Bleak House kind of fog: the sort of fog that is made denser by the multiplication of organizations. The town parson's job is a matter of opening eyes, of getting people to look at and into the way of life that the modern city is fashioning for people to live. It is a new way of life and we need all the sensitised comment upon it that we can possibly muster. He, the parson, will need to see it, and get others to see it, through a bi-focal medium; one frame of which is supplied by realistic assessment of what is actually experienced, and the other by Christian hope, compassion, conviction and reflection.

This calls for the transformation of the parson into a creature more personally involved than he has been for a long time. His job in the great town agglomerations, which threaten to depersonalize, is to foster the whole process by which personal life is laid hold of, nurtured, encouraged and extended. He can only do this with any degree of the particularity that it demands with a small body of people. He cannot do it in any short-term engagement with them. The increasing mobility, the almost nomadic character of a good deal of town life, makes it all the more necessary that some stable relationships are being fostered and maintained within it. Whoever else goes, he must stay; and he must stay, not bewailing the past glories and the disappearance of familiar things, but still expectant of a new theophany, still open-eyed and receptive, always rebuilding the worn fabric of personal life which it is the job of the Church to maintain. What matters here is the kind of identity which the church body is trying to live by. It can have none other that merits devotion than a willingness to be constantly reborn. It is the parson's job to redirect it continually to those harsh conditions which promise nothing but exact everything.

There remains a sphere within all this which can only be called "spirituality", and it calls for the working out in town life, in the midst of the great "town's harsh heart-wearying roar", of the equivalent of that gracious "so cool, so calm, so bright" way of living that Herbert wrote about. The parson is not the only one called upon to attempt this, but he has a special commitment to it. It is his job to distil from these raw unlikely conditions those perceptions which are transfiguring, redemptive, energizing, by and through the interplay of his own ministry with the work of other men. That is why he can never cease from visiting those endless rows of terraced houses, backyards, shops, detached houses, because without this he cannot know and be known. He has to learn to accompany people rather than to try to direct them. The dwellers in cities are already too much accustomed to being pushed or cajoled into this or that "lane". What most of us need now is the presence of someone who shows that he understands where our pilgrimage has reached, who knows what a dead end it so often appears to be, but who illuminates a yard or so of it so that we take heart and tread it out more hopefully.

I3

The Country Parson

J. H. B. ANDREWS

There shall be joy in heaven over one sinner that repenteth. – St Luke 15:7

We minister to souls. Souls! Methinks in that one word there is a sermon. Immortal souls! Precious souls! One whereof is more worth than all the world besides, the price of the blood of the Son of God.

> – George Bull, Bishop of St. David's
> *A Companion for the Candidates of Holy Orders* (1714),
> reprinted in *The Clergyman's Instructor* (1807).

The country parson has for some years now enjoyed a poor "image". He is thought to have nothing to do. His work does not keep him "at full stretch". While his brethren in the towns are struggling, sometimes "single-handed", with tens of thousands, he counts his population in hundreds. He is a glaring example of the Church's misdirected manpower. He is an anachronism, a relic of the time when the economy of the nation was predominantly rural and immobile. He is burdened moreover with an unhappy inheritance from the past, for his predecessors are widely thought to have been men unmindful of their spiritual duties, who lived for hunting and amusement, in league with, and usually related to, the squire (another much misjudged person). The "hunting squarson" is widely thought to have been typical of the eighteenth and early nineteenth centuries.

This article is not an historical study, and yet a sound historical basis is necessary in trying to assess the present and future role of the country clergyman. It is true of him as of others that the "evil that men do lives after them, The good is oft interred with their bones". The good is indeed sometimes recorded on marble, but few read the epitaph, and when they do so they reflect with Dr Johnson that "in lapidary inscriptions a man is not upon oath".

As previously noted in THEOLOGY[1], the chance survival of the sermons of two obscure and ordinary clergymen affords an opportunity of verifying the epitaph. The sermons prove that these men were indeed "zealous dispensers of the Word", and other records prove that they testified "their love for their Redeemer by feeding the hungry and clothing the naked". Their task, between the years 1803 to 1841, did not seem to them to be easy. It was an age, as they put it, of schism and infidelity. Their ministry included the years of the Napoleonic wars and the years of depression which followed, when many were on parish relief and desperate men took to riot and arson. It is impossible to say how representative these two clergymen were, but they serve to rebuke hasty generalizations.

Surveying the long list of his predecessors, the country incumbent is justified in assuming that they were virtuous men. He may recall that whereas Chaucer satirizes the monk and the friar, and in a gentler way the prioress, he chooses for encomium the "povre Persoun of a toun". The parson was virtuous, and he was not idle.

> Wyd was his parisshe, and houses far a-sonder,
> But he ne lafte nat, for reyn ne thonder,
> In siknes nor in meschief, to visyte
> The ferreste in his parisshe, muche and lyte,
> Up-on his feet, and in his hand a staf.

This parson was well known to be the plowman's brother. The social status of the clergy has been much misjudged. Macaulay says of the early eighteenth-century country clergyman that his "sacerdotal office" was "his single title to reverence", and that his place in the big house was in the servants' hall rather than in the drawing-room. As for devotion to his spiritual duties, perhaps John Wesley's testimony may be taken as well informed and unbiased, and as applying equally to town and country:

> They [the clergy of his day] have not only more learning of the most valuable kind, but abundantly much more religion. Insomuch that the English and Irish Clergy are generally allowed to be not inferior to any in Europe, for piety as well as for knowledge.[2]

There were wealthy livings, some very wealthy, but the majority were poor, many so poor that they did not provide a living, and must be held in plurality, as Mr Irwine the rector of Broxton held also the vicarages of Hayslope and Blythe. The Victorians succeeded, widely but not universally, in restoring the ideal of the incumbent resident on his cure, providing every Sunday the full services of the Church for every rural community. It was done by supplementing the revenues of the benefice from the incumbent's own pocket. Fifty years ago a church-warden would say to the patron, "It is useless for a man to think of coming

[1] October 1967, pp. 451 ff.
[2] Sermon CVIII, *Of Attending the Church Services.*

here unless he has private means". But those who remember the clergy of fifty years ago will remember that not all of them had private means, and that there was no such thing as a social status of the clergy as such. Some were much more at ease in the servants' hall than in the drawing-room.

The change which has come over the clergy in the last half century has nothing to do with their own social status. The change is in society. The clergy are no longer needed to supply recommends for hospitals, to supervise clothing clubs, and to provide the only entertainment which the villagers could enjoy. Adequate wages and State welfare supply these needs. The country clergyman is left much more to his own proper work.

But is there still work for him to do? Unless his parish happens to be in an area of industrial or residential development it will have barely half the population of the mid-nineteenth century; and yet it will still be greater than that of the mid-fifteenth century, when as likely as not his church was either rebuilt or enlarged. The following are estimated or actual figures for one small parish: 1524, 168; 1569, 135; 1642, 258; 1851, 394, 1961, 173. The corresponding figures for a larger neighbour are: 458; 486; 1,029; 1,494; 720. But this latter parish was thought to need an assistant curate (paid by the patron) when its population was over a thousand. Judged by the standards of the past there is still work to do, if population alone is the basis.

It must follow that if there is no longer sufficient work for the country parson to do, it must be either because people's needs are no longer what they were, or because the clergy feel that it is no longer their duty to find out and meet those needs. It seems to be true that the modern clergyman is not as much in the homes of his people as his predecessors were, although personal problems are no less acute in this present age. From a sermon of a young clergyman preaching in 1811 it is clear that the pastoral visit was regarded as an opportunity of personal exhortation and instruction, supplementing what was given in church. Twice yearly in the 1830s the curate of Culmstock would take prayers, with an exposition of Scripture, in each household in the parish, unless the householder declined to admit him for such a purpose.[1] Methods of the past cannot be applied to modern conditions, but it is beyond dispute that even in a small community there are many personal spiritual problems which only patient personal knowledge will discover. Organizations and a duplicated news-sheet are no substitute.

The country clergy of the last century deplored the lack of response to their private and public ministrations, in terms almost identical with those of their successors, but they did not complain of having too little to do, neither did they regard their talents or time as wasted. It is possible that they regarded themselves as ordained to be rather than to do, to fill a

[1] *Memoirs of Frederick Temple*, ed. E. G. Sandford, I., p. 27.

unique place in the community rather than to fill their own time with activity. Undoubtedly some of them benefited the whole Church by their writings, as did R. W. Church when he was for twenty years rector of the small Somerset parish of Whatley. But he also published his village sermons; he left the parish with great reluctance, and his devotion to his parishioners was signified by his burial among them, although he had left the parish many years before. Bishop E. S. Talbot used to speak with admiration and affection for R. S. Hunt, who devoted the whole of his ministry to the 300 people of Markbeech, in Kent, and he sent his own sons to him for preparation for Confirmation. The decrease in the value of parochial endowments and the fall in the number of clergy make such ministries, at least for the foreseeable future, extremely rare, but this does not mean that the priest so employed would be "wasted".

It may be said that the Church always succumbs to the ways of the world. The present age has been one of planning. Therefore the Church must "plan" and be concerned with "strategy". It is also an age which is vitally concerned with productivity. Therefore the Church must deploy its manpower to the best advantage. This is easily said, but there are no criteria upon which to base the redeployment. The most obvious remedy is to distribute the clergy equally amongst the people.

But people live in communities, some large, some small, some parochial, some non-parochial. A community may be a college, a school, a hospital, a regiment, a ship. A priest is not thought to be wasted because the members of such communities are numbered in hundreds rather than in thousands. The community is felt to be incomplete without him, that is, without a man who is himself a member of the community, ordained to be the minister of word and sacrament, and appointed to be its spiritual pastor.

The country parish, it is said, has ceased to be a community. It has lost the leadership of the big house (in the minority of parishes which had one), it has lost its school and its schoolmaster. Its resident village policeman has been replaced by a radio-controlled motor-cyclist. It is true that much has been lost, notably the power of self-government, but recent years have seen the growth and almost universal spread of new institutions – Women's Institutes, Young Farmers' Clubs, and village halls. A Young Farmers' Club dinner and dance, even when relatives and friends swell the numbers to 200, has very much the aspect of a family reunion, and the vicar will be provided with a complimentary ticket. *The Times* of 28 September 1968 carried an extended article under the significant title "The Living Village".[1] Even in parishes with populations below 400 there will be youth clubs and clubs for the over-60s, where there is anyone to give a lead. The country incumbent cannot but reflect

[1] Based on a book, subsequently published, under the same title, by Paul Jennings.

with interest that, whereas he sees elaborate club premises in towns either closed or almost deserted after initial periods of prosperity, his own club, with but little to offer, and with only his own inexpert guidance, goes on. The boys have motor-cycles or cars as soon as the law permits, and go far afield for a dance, but they still like to meet with their own neighbours for "club" once a week. And the old folk much prefer a Christmas party in their own village hall, run by their own more agile neighbours, rather than go and join with strangers in the town.

There is still community life, but the modern community does not always fit in with the boundaries of an ancient parish, neither is the ancient parish church always well placed to serve the needs of the modern community. But as far as possible the people must meet for worship where they normally meet for their daily business and social purposes, for it is unnatural for them to do otherwise. To abandon the community's place of worship on any Sunday, and to convey the faithful few to a "centre", is to deny to them their proper function and privilege of witnessing to the things of God within their own community, and is the way to destroy the parish church. The strain upon the country parson is not in the numbers – indeed his work would be easier if he had more people – neither (unless he is an old man) is it in the travelling, but in putting himself into the life, circumstances and problems of a second, and maybe of a third, community.

In one respect at least a modern incumbent is better off than his recent predecessors. Financial problems are now easier than they have been at any time since the abolition of the compulsory church rate in 1868. Wealthy parishioners did not always give generously, and other country parishioners had very little to give. In 1890 one parish which had a resident and wealthy church-going patron showed a deficit of £2 6s. 5d. in total church expenses of £4 12s. 6d. At this same period a larger neighbouring parish always had a deficit, made good year after year first by the vicar and then by a farmer churchwarden, despite a big house employing fourteen servants. Its total church expenses seldom exceeded £30. Today in both these parishes there is no lack of money, whether for ordinary expenses, for fabric repair, or for missions. It is customary to speak of church repair as a burden grievous to be borne; in fact it is a challenge to which the people will rise.

Country parishes are almost infinitely various. Some are indeed so depopulated that they have ceased to be communities. This is nothing new. It happened in the fifteenth century, and it happened later, and our predecessors were content to let such churches die a natural death. They did not plan their extinction, neither did they artificially prolong their life. Other parishes are being transformed by industrial or residential development. The majority have been suffering from a fall in population which has perhaps now reached its nadir. Judged by standards of productivity the incumbents of such parishes will fare badly. They cannot show as many Confirmation candidates or as many Easter communicants per priest as their town brethren. In return for the money spent on their preparation for the ministry there is little to show. Perhaps a ruthless business organization would cut off the country parson as unproductive.

What is to be the criterion? If one immortal soul is really precious in the sight of God, then the country parson is just as fully justified in 1969 as in any preceding year. The soul can only be known to the pastor who lives in, or is able to make himself a member of, the community. Such knowledge requires patience. An impatient commercial traveller was once heard to lament that it took him seven times as long to see his clients in the country as in the town. (It is probably as easy for a priest to minister to a compact town parish of 5,000 as to a scattered country one of 700.) But the priest who feels himself called of God to this uniquely important task of his cure of souls must never be impatient. His text must be, "Woe unto you that have lost your patience!" He must be content to let patience have her perfect work. And if he is patient he will have his reward. A little of the joy that is in heaven over one sinner that repenteth will be his when he sees one of his parishioners, after twenty years of indifference, turn to the worship and service of God and find the joy that is in so doing. He will of course reflect that God could have worked without him, but he will nevertheless justifiably presume that his twenty years of patience had not been in vain.

14

The Available Priesthood

J. DOMINIAN

What does it mean to be a priest? The word priest comes from the Greek *presbyteros* which means an elder, someone who may enter the presence of God, speak directly to him, offer himself in sacrifice to him.

Fundamental to the Judaeo-Christian tradition is the belief that God exists, has revealed himself, and has created man. However interpreted there is a further basic belief, namely that the initial harmonious relationship between God and man was destroyed after the Fall. In this estrangement mediation was necessary and the priesthood became an institute for mediation. In the Old Testament the functions of the priest included delivering an oracle, giving and explaining the law or the Torah and presenting to God the prayers and petitions of the faithful. Thus he represented God before men and also men before God. He was an intermediary and in the words of the Epistle to the Hebrews, "Every high priest has been taken out of mankind and is appointed to act for men in their relations to God, to offer gifts and sacrifices for sins".

The high priest of the New Testament is Christ, the Son of God who, in obedience to the Father, came into the world to take flesh and offer himself as the perfect mediator to his father. Thus all priesthood thereafter must take its central meaning from the priesthood of Christ. His words and deeds are the sources of all priesthood actualized in his life, death, resurrection and ascension. Before leaving the world he served, Christ instituted the Church, that body of people who were to continue his presence mystically in the world, and in that Church the Roman Catholic tradition has delineated two senses of the priesthood: a general priesthood in which all of us through baptism share in the priesthood of Christ, and a more specific one, the ordained priesthood specifically entrusted with a special mission.

In the Decree on the Ministry and Life of Priests in Vatican II the purpose of the priest is described thus:

The purpose, therefore, which priests pursue by their ministry and life is the glory of God the Father as it is to be achieved in Christ. . . . Hence whether engaged in prayer and adoration, preaching the Word, offering the Eucharistic sacrifice, ministering the other sacraments, or performing any of the work of the ministry for men, priests are contributing to the extension of God's Glory as well as to the development of divine life in men.

Prayer, preaching the word, celebrating the sacraments, in brief, are the instruments of making Christ present in the world. Christ is the head of the body, is the sacrament, the source of divine life which as a sacred reality is actualized in the various sacraments, the central one being the Holy Eucharist. In the mass the priest with the people, acting in the person of Christ, offers to the Father the perfect sacrifice of the Cross, the perpetual event of reconciliation between man and God, and makes available to us truly the body and blood of Our Lord which, as in the last supper, is given freely to all of us. By taking the host and drinking the blood we, in Freudian terms, incorporate God within us, an incorporation whose mystery is beyond understanding but whose reality is an abundance of love. The mass is a perpetual reminder of Christ's availability, an availability which the priest must make his own before and after each mass if he is to follow in the footsteps of the Lord. This availability has to be reassessed afresh in each successive age; and I should like to suggest to those who fear for the future of the priesthood that its continuity is safely enshrined in its origin, but its actualization must take constant heed lest it abandons the prototype of the Lord.

And so the priest's availability must be considered in relation to the needs of the day. It is not only availability in time and place that is needed. This is vital; but the quality of it is just as important. In an age profoundly preoccupied with the realization of man's highest potential, physically and psychologically, the priest must lend himself to respond creatively to the needs of those who long to fulfill the image of God in themselves. This is an age acutely aware of its aspiration to creation, not to condemnation, and we can be reminded of Christ's non-judgmental availability to all those who sought their perfection however badly they had fared in the process of their personal growth. St John puts these words in the mouth of Our Lord: "You judge by human standards, I judge no one." Here the word "judge" is used in the semitic sense: I condemn no one.

Without condemning, but not ignoring, human imperfection Christ seeks the person's *metanoia*, his change of mind away from personal disintegration towards wholeness. Thus the non-judgmental availability has the specific purpose of healing the wounds of human weakness in the sacrament of penance. But, like the Holy Eucharist, this process of healing must extend before and beyond the sacramental focus.

To his non-judgmental availability present in his everyday relationships Christ added a divine empathy, once again portrayed with a stunning brevity in the Gospel of St John. Christ "could tell what a man had in him". Empathy means the capacity to identify, and identify with, the inner needs of men and women struggling to discover and transform themselves. The priest today must learn how to enter into empathetic relationships based on authentic understanding of man's deep advance into an awareness of his complex self.

The sacraments have been correctly held to be of the greatest importance in the Christian life as crucial contacts with the life of Christ, vital source of grace. But their meaning is enhanced both for the priest and for the people if the Christian life leading up to and flowing from them is an extension of Christ's presence. The nearer the priest's relationship with people can imitate the empathetic, non-judgmental availability of Christ the greater will become Christ's presence in the world. But if the priest is to employ himself repeatedly as Christ did in this type of availability, then he needs the support of the rest of the Christian community to be replenished. If our priests are to nurture us in the way suggested, we have to nurture them. The priest is set apart as Christ set himself apart: the priest becomes one of us as Christ became one with us. Together, priests and layman, all Christians become what Peter described, a chosen race, a royal priesthood, a concentrated nation, a people set apart to sing the praises of God who called us out of darkness into his wonderful light.